WALKING WELLINGTON

Walking Wellington

23 WALKS OF DISCOVERY IN AND AROUND WELLINGTON

KATHY OMBLER

This edition published in 2008 by New Holland Publishers (NZ) Ltd
Auckland • Sydney • London • Cape Town

www.newhollandpublishers.co.nz

218 Lake Road, Northcote, Auckland 0627, New Zealand
Unit 1, 66 Gibbes Street, Chatswood, NSW 2067, Australia
86–88 Edgware Road, London W2 2EA, United Kingdom
80 McKenzie Street, Cape Town 8001, South Africa

First published in 2001 by New Holland Publishers (NZ) Ltd
Copyright © 2008 in text: Kathy Ombler
Copyright © 2008 in maps: New Holland Publishers (NZ) Ltd
Copyright © 2008 New Holland Publishers (NZ) Ltd

Publishing manager: Christine Thomson
Editor: Renée Lang
Layout: Justine Mackenzie
Cover illustration: Sue Reidy
Maps: Pauline Whimp

National Library of New Zealand Cataloguing-in-Publication Data

Ombler, Kathy.
Walking Wellington : 23 walks of discovery in and around
Wellington / author, Kathy Ombler ; maps, Pauline Whimp.
New ed. with updated walks.
Previous ed.: 2001.
ISBN 978-1-86966-227-1
1. Trails—New Zealand—Wellington—Guidebooks. 2. Trails—
New Zealand—Wellington (Region)—Guidebooks.
3. Wellington (N.Z.)—Guidebooks. 4. Wellington (N.Z. : Region)
—Guidebooks. I. Whimp, Pauline. II. Title.
919.3604—dc 22

10 9 8 7 6 5 4 3 2

Colour reproduction by Image Centre Ltd., Auckland
Printed by Times Offset (M) Sdn Bhd, Malaysia, on paper sourced from sustainable forests.

All rights reserved. No part of this publication may be reproduced, stored in a retrieval
system, or transmitted in any form or by any means, electronic, mechanical, photocopying,
recording or otherwise, without the prior permission of the publishers and copyright holders.

While the author and publishers have made every effort to ensure the information in this
book was correct at the time of going to press, they accept no responsibility for any errors
that may have occurred or for any injury or inconvenience that may result from following
the information contained herein. Facilities, locations, or amenities can change over time, so
it is recommended that the reader call the operator or service and confirm any information
that might be required.

'Will our descendants prize this unique heritage from the dim past,
and preserve these sanctuaries intact?'
Leonard Cockayne

This walking guide is dedicated to the countless volunteers throughout
the greater Wellington region who, individually or in environmental groups,
devote so much time and energy to restoring and safeguarding
our natural heritage.

ACKNOWLEDGEMENTS

Many people in Wellington have a great knowledge and love of the region's natural and human heritage. The author wishes to thank the following for their assistance and advice.

Anita Benbrook, Derek Thompson, Mike Oates and Dave Halliday (Wellington City Council); Kelly Crandle and Rebecca Hobbs (Hutt City Council); Andrew Gray (Porirua City Council); Ruth Barrett (Porirua Library); Nola Urquhart, Matt Ballantine, Chris Wootton, John Bissell, Graham Laws, Susan Edwards, Steve Edwards and Gareth Cooper (Greater Wellington Regional Council); Jeremy Rolfe, Ian Cooksley, Wayne Boness and Waikanae area office staff (Department of Conservation); Raewyn Epsom (Karori Sanctuary); Geoff Chapple (Te Araroa, the Long Pathway); and staff of Petone Settlers Museum and Positively Wellington Tourism. Also Jan and Arnold Heine, Brian Fisher, Dave Hansford, Marieke Hilhorst, Chris Horne, Bill Wrightson, Bob Box, Rei Ahipene Mercer and John, Jenny, Sally and Kate Ombler.

CONTENTS

Introduction 9
About Wellington 10
Using this book 13
Getting around 14
Map of Wellington 15

Wellington waterfront: Heritage buildings and maritime meanderings 17

Molesworth to Mulgrave: The seat of government 24

Civic Square to Courtenay Place: Civic pride in the café capital 32

Zealandia – The Karori Sanctuary Experience: A remarkable conservation story 39

Otari-Wilton's Bush: A native botanical garden 46

Ngaio Gorge/Trelissick Park: The greening of a shady gully 53

Skyline Track: Stunning views and windy walking 59

Old Coach Road: Gently graded country heritage 66

Southern Walkway: From harbour haven to stormy south coast 70

Southern Miramar Peninsula: A peninsula for penguins 76

Makara Track: A walk on the wild side 82

Petone Esplanade: History, harbour and heaps of fun 88

Korokoro Valley: The hidden glen 94

Belmont Trig: Beautiful bush and inspiring views   **99**

Days Bay: Beech trees, rata and orchids   **105**

Butterfly Creek: Of beech forest and Butterfly Creek   **111**

Pencarrow Head: Lighthouses, lakes and a long coastal walk   **116**

Kaitoke: Big trees, big river   **123**

Colonial Knob: Forest and fantastic views   **129**

Wairaka Point: A coastal journey   **136**

Battle Hill: Farm, forest and a battle story   **142**

Queen Elizabeth Park: Walking in the dunelands   **147**

Kapiti Island: Walking with the birds   **153**

Further reading   **160**

INTRODUCTION

From the vibrancy of the city's downtown, to the quiet of a forest-filled valley, to the roar of wild surf crashing over coastal rocks – when writing a walking guide for Wellington one is spoiled for choice. Within these pages 23 walks explore a collection of the city's finest natural landscapes, cityscapes and heritage features, delve into some hidden spots, and roam into regional parks and reserves.

The people of Wellington are passionate about their city. It usually takes little time for newcomers to understand why, at which point they inevitably become staunch defenders of the place. They talk of the beauty of the harbour, the heart and soul of the city, the hills and forest-filled valleys within the city limits, and the wild and wonderful coastline.

Wellington people are also passionate walkers. Be it a commuting walk from suburban home to city office or a weekend wander further afield, be it into the teeth of a northerly or on a calm, clear capital day, walkers are always out and about. The hills don't seem to matter – in fact with elevation come gloriously expanding views of the harbour and the city and beyond to forest-covered ranges, the Marlborough Sounds and Kaikoura mountains.

Wellington, one of New Zealand's oldest cities, has since 1865 been the seat of parliament, and many fine historic buildings are visited on walks in this book. These buildings are well cared for, and so too is the natural landscape. Otari-Wilton's Bush and Karori Sanctuary, within the city bounds, are two outstanding examples of Wellington's traditional conservation ethic. Regional parks and Department of Conservation reserves protect a multitude of natural features and landscapes and are blessed with fine networks of paths and tracks.

Join me, then, for a tour of grand heritage buildings, cafés, museums, harbour views, native forests, sheltered valleys, windswept ridges, wetlands, native birdsong, lighthouses, sea cliffs, rocky shorelines, boulder-strewn beaches and one very special island wildlife sanctuary.

ABOUT WELLINGTON

The earliest name for Wellington is Te Upoko o te Ika a Maui, which means the head of Maui's fish.

Legend tells that Wellington Harbour was once a lake inhabited by two taniwha. One, named Ngake, longed for the freedom of the open sea. The taniwha smashed a passage through to Raukawamoana (Cook Strait), thus creating the harbour entrance plied by ships and ferries today.

The second taniwha, Whataitai, tried to escape on the other side of Motu Kairanga (Miramar Peninsula). He pushed off with his tail but before he reached the open sea was caught by the receding tide. His body forms the isthmus where the airport is located, now known as the suburb of Hataitai.

The Polynesian explorer Kupe called into the harbour and landed on the Seatoun foreshore, which he named Te Turanga o Kupe. His explorations included the coast near Porirua. Kupe is credited with naming Kapiti and Mana Islands, as well as Porirua, a name that means 'two flowings of the tide' and refers to the adjacent Pauatahanui and Porirua inlets.

The coastal area around Porirua was one of the first settled in the Wellington region; Paremata has been settled since about AD 1450 when the harbours, the ready availability of food in the sea and the coastal forests were prime attractions for early settlers. The Maori name for Wellington Harbour, Whanganui a Tara (the great harbour of Tara), comes from the people of Tara, who moved to the area from Mahia Peninsula. Ngati Tara and Ngati Ira were the established Wellington tribes until the 1800s, when Te Atiawa and Ngati Toa from Taranaki moved south and took over the region. Today a complex, unique mix of iwi live in Wellington, though Te Atiawa are the recognised tangata whenua. In the area around Porirua and the Kapiti Coast, Ngati Toa are tangata whenua.

Europeans first established their presence as whalers on the Kapiti Coast and Kapiti Island in the early 1800s. In Wellington, it was the arrival in 1840 of the New Zealand Company ship Aurora, with its complement of British settlers, that marked the start of the capital's development. Initial plans to establish a town on the swampy flats of Pito-one (Petone) were abandoned when the Heretaunga (now called Hutt River) flooded, and the settlers shifted their development plans across the harbour to Thorndon.

It is well known that Wellington sits directly over a major fault line, and in 1855 the earth moved dramatically! One of the biggest earthquakes in New Zealand's history shook the fledgling settlement and raised land around the harbour by about a metre, draining the Te Aro swamp (now Courtenay Place) and creating more land for development and for a road linking Wellington with Hutt Valley. The earthquake also drained coastal swamps around the Hutt River mouth, lagoons on Miramar Peninsula and exposed mudflats at Pauatahanui.

Humans created more uplift with reclamation that has added more than 155 hectares to the inner city area, and much of downtown Wellington sits on land that was initially underwater or in swamp.

While most of Wellington's original forest cover has been cleared or burned, significant stands of mature native trees remain, and vast areas are clothed in a mantle of healthy, fast-growing regeneration, some upwards of 100 years old. In her book *Wellington's Living Cloak* botanist Isobel Gabites wrote that Wellington contains one of the most wide-ranging and fascinating living textbooks of botany in the country. 'The dramatically varied landscape . . . creates a pot pourri of plant habitats,' she wrote, mentioning examples such as 'groves of karaka tucked into gullies, springy cushions of pohuehue on the coast and beech forests not twenty minutes' drive from the capital'.

Today, Wellington is blessed with a literal army of volunteers and environmental watchdog groups that work with councils in the cause of forest restoration and protection. Armed with chainsaws, axes, slashers and grubbers, they have toiled against introduced weeds; they have raised native seedlings and planted thousands of trees and shrubs in valleys and on hillsides; they have rallied against animal pests, such as possums, and they have waged paper wars on environmental policy matters. And they continue to do these things.

Officially, the future seems to be in good hands. The Greater Wellington Regional Council has set aside millions of dollars for environmental enhancement and with the Department of Conservation continues to battle animal pests. The Wellington, Hutt, Upper Hutt, Porirua and Kapiti Coast councils are constantly developing and upgrading their walking track networks.

There are many more delightful walks throughout the Wellington region that could have been included in a guide such as this. The 23 walks here have been selected for their outstanding natural, scenic, historic and cultural qualities, and because they offer a selection of the special landscapes and features inherent in the region. Not for nothing is Wellington also referred to as New Zealand's cultural and café capital. As well as natural features you will find heritage buildings, theatres, museums, galleries, designer shops, and of course a wonderful blend of ethnic and New Zealand cafés, restaurants and bars along the walks in this book.

If you thought Wellington was about grey suits, bureaucrats, wind and gorse then take this book, walk the walks, and you will surely think again.

WALK MAP KEY
S Walk start   **F** Walk finish   **P** Parking area   **T** Public toilets
Please note that the maps are not all to the same scale.

USING THIS BOOK

DISTANCE/TIME
The times given are only a guide – obviously they will vary depending on people's fitness. They may also be different from the signs on the ground.

WHAT TO EXPECT UNDERFOOT
I have endeavoured to describe the surface and slope of each walk so that people with wheelchairs can judge whether they can be managed.

DOGS
Most dog owners know *their* dog is perfect. Nevertheless, dog restrictions are put in place for good reasons, such as safeguarding native wildlife and farm animals. Please follow the rules!

MOUNTAIN BIKES
Don't be deterred if a route is a dual walking/biking track. Mountain biking is particularly popular in Wellington and most bikers are grateful for off-road opportunities and are considerate of other users.

PRIVATE LAND
Please respect the generosity of landowners of private land: leave gates as found, stay away from stock and adhere to access restrictions during lambing season.

PEST CONTROL
Signs will warn where pest control operations are being undertaken. Wherever you are, leave any animals alone, dead or alive.

BROCHURES
Most walks in this book are well described, in part or all, in brochures provided by local councils and the Department of Conservation. These are regularly updated and available at visitor centres and libraries throughout the region.

GETTING AROUND

Many of the walks in this book are well served by public transport, be it bus, train or harbour ferry. Most walks are loops, or of an out-and-back nature. Where the walks do not start and finish in the same place you will need to ferry two cars or catch a bus or train back to your starting point (or to where your car is parked, or home – whichever suits). In the case of the inner-city walks this is particularly easy; for those further afield you might prefer to organise two cars or a pick-up or drop-off with obliging friends. I have endeavoured to clarify your options in each walk description.

For all bus and train services, call Greater Wellington's Metlink service centre on 0-4-801 700 or visit www.metlink.org.nz

For the East by West Ferry (Wellington City to Days Bay and Petone) phone 0-4-499 1282 or visit www.eastbywest.co.nz

WELLINGTON WALKS

1. Wellington city walks:
   Wellington waterfront;
   Molesworth to Mulgrave;
   Civic Square to Courtenay Place
2. Karori Sanctuary
3. Otari-Wilton's Bush
4. Ngaio Gorge/Trelissick Park
5. Skyline Track
6. Old Coach Road
7. Southern Walkway
8. Southern Miramar Peninsula
9. Makara Track
10. Petone Esplanade
11. Belmont Regional Park walks:
    Korokoro Valley; Belmont Trig
12. Days Bay
13. Butterfly Creek
14. Pencarrow Head
15. Kaitoke
16. Colonial Knob
17. Wairaka Point
18. Battle Hill
19. Queen Elizabeth Park
20. Kapiti Island

Legend

- REGIONAL PARKS, RESERVES & BUSH
- **1** MAIN ROUTES
- **7** WALKS

Map Labels

Waikanae
Kapiti Island
Paraparaumu
Paekakariki
Pukerua Bay
Pakuratahi Forks
TARARUA FOREST PARK
Mana Island
Plimmerton
Pauatahanui
PORIRUA
TAWA
UPPER HUTT
LOWER HUTT
PETONE
Somes (Matiu) Island
WELLINGTON
RIMUTAKA FOREST PARK

16 WALKING WELLINGTON

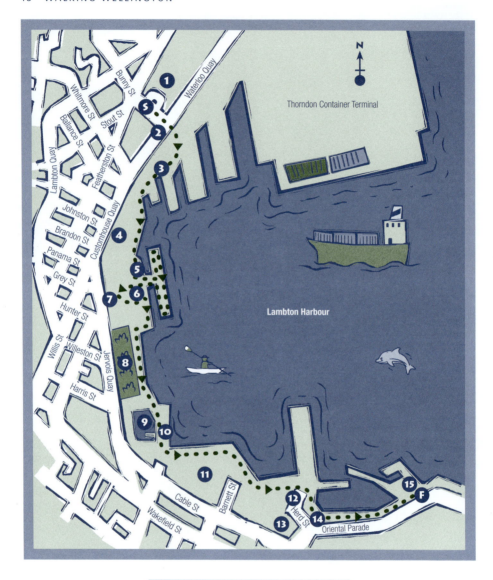

WALK KEY

1. Wellington railway station 2. Shed 21/Waterloo on Quay
3. Old Ferry Building 4. Sheds 11 & 13 5. Shed 5 6. Queens Wharf
7. Museum of Wellington 8. Frank Kitts Park 9. Lagoon
10. Taranaki Wharf 11. Te Papa Tongarewa 12. Chaffers Dock
13. Waitangi Park 14. Clyde Quay 15. Freyberg Pool and Fitness Centre

WELLINGTON WATERFRONT

Heritage buildings and maritime meanderings

Wellington's harbour is what makes Wellington city. Historically, it is the city's *raison d'être*. Today the harbour, backed with villas and bush-covered hills, creates a spectacle that is admired by both Wellingtonians and visitors from around the world.

So what better way to experience the visual delights and heritage of Wellington city than to take a stroll above the downtown Lambton Harbour waterfront. With city office towers on one side and the sparkling harbour on the other – and a blend of heritage buildings, museums, parks and open spaces, cafés, restaurants and entertainment along the way – the waterfront is sacrosanct to Wellingtonians. Council development plans for the area are watched closely and are inevitably the subject of vociferous public debate.

START
Wellington railway station

FINISH
Freyberg Pool and Fitness Centre

DISTANCE/TIME
2.2 km, 1–2 hours (one-way)

ACCESS
This downtown Wellington walk is accessible via all major bus routes as well as by rail.

WHAT TO EXPECT UNDERFOOT
Wharves and city footpaths, no hills

DOGS
Prohibited from Oriental Bay all hours, elsewhere prohibited 8 am–6 pm

BIKES
Yes – lots – plus inline skaters, skateboarders and even quadricycles!

Full details of the history of the Lambton Harbour waterfront, its days as Wellington's port and its historic buildings, can be found in Wellington City Council's *Maritime Heritage Trail* brochure, available from council visitor information centres.

Our time for this walk allows for a leisurely stroll, however it doesn't take into account stops you may wish to make at the numerous attractions along the way.

THE WALK

We start at one of the capital city's landmark buildings, the ❶ **Wellington railway station**. Built during the Depression, at the time of its completion in 1937 it was New Zealand's largest public building. A more recent addition, on the lawn in front of the station, is the Mahatma Ghandi statue, by sculptor Gautam Pal, presented in 2007 by the Indian Council for Cultural Relations to recognise the example set by New Zealand of being a tolerant, open and inclusive society. The statue's location was chosen to acknowledge Ghandi as a man of the people and one who used public transport to travel.

From the front of the station, cross Waterloo Quay at the lights near the corner of Bunny Street and walk to the left of and behind the two-storey brick building of ❷ **Shed 21/Waterloo on Quay**. This former wharf storage shed, built in 1911 as a wool store and now housing apartments and office space, has a Category One rating with the Historic Places Trust.

Away to the left is the sprawling expanse of Wellington's port. Port activities were originally centred closer to the city at Queens Wharf, but the advent of container shipping and the need for space saw the port shift northwards to its present Thorndon location. In 1870, 58 trading vessels called into Queens Wharf; Wellington's port now handles 4500 shipping movements each year.

Heading away from the port and crossing open space brings you to the ❸ **Old Ferry Building**. This little two-storeyed weatherboard building was for 38 years the ticket office for the Eastbourne ferry service. Behind the Old Ferry Building, the *Lady Elizabeth III* police launch is likely to be resting at its dock, waiting for the next sea rescue mission. When the wharves here were busier the police had a much larger presence on the waterfront, with foreshore police numbers peaking at 23 in the 1940s. An old red buoy resting on the wharf is one of several navigational buoys that have washed ashore over the years. An information board here recounts much of historical significance, including pre-reclamation Maori history.

ESSENTIAL WELLINGTON

Veer left by the buoy and follow the waterfront, past the berths of harbour cruise and deep-sea fishing vessels and artwork celebrating the wharf history. Old wharf sheds and corporate office towers on the right offer a visual contrast with the open waters on the left, with the villas of Oriental Bay and slopes of Mt Victoria providing yet another contrast across the harbour. This is essential Wellington.

Stay close to the water's edge. Red-billed gulls (tarapunga) may be watching your progress, ready to fly from their bollard perch should you offer them a hint of a food scrap.

The contrasts continue as you near the Meridian Energy building, completed in 2007 and reportedly one of New Zealand's first purpose-built 'green' office buildings, which is located close to ❹ **Sheds 11 and 13**, two near-identical historic wharf buildings. In the early 1900s these Edwardian Industrial style sheds sat at the harbour's edge – the wharf area you are walking on is just one of the major reclamations undertaken in Wellington city. Shed 13 is now a coffee roastery, Shed 11 is used for functions and art exhibitions.

As you approach Queens Wharf the incongruous mix of buildings continues. Directly ahead is the grand old ❺ **Shed 5**, of 1886 vintage, formerly a timber warehouse and now a restaurant and the oldest building on the waterfront. Next door, jutting out across the water, is Shed 3, now better known as the Dockside Restaurant and Bar, which started life, also as a timber warehouse, in 1887.

By now you will have come across some 'sculptural prose', the first of several thoughtful quotations by well-known New Zealand writers incorporated in the Wellington Writers Walk along the waterfront.

Continue your walk between Shed 5 and Dockside, for there is much exploring to be done in and around ❻ **Queens Wharf**.

On the open wharf old cranes give a hint of what this area once looked like, and underneath an old straddle carrier a large shipping container houses a static display of the history of Wellington's waterfront. Visiting navy ships, small cruise liners and luxury yachts sometimes moor at the wharf.

On a good-weather day sea kayakers may be nosing around, exploring the eerie waterways that extend for several hundred metres underneath the wharves. Many of these kayaks will come from Ferg's Rock 'n' Kayak, an adventure business established in Shed 6 by Olympic gold-medal paddler Ian Ferguson. Inside, a climbing wall provides challenges for all ages as well as great spectator fun.

History and culture come to the fore on the city side of Queens Wharf. The New Zealand Academy of Fine Arts, which holds regular exhibitions, is housed in what was the Wharf Office. This late English Classical style building was designed in 1896 by the well-known Frederick de Jersey Clere. Take time to read the delightful story of Paddy the Wanderer inscribed on a plaque on the front of this building.

On the south side of the great wrought-iron gates that have guarded this wharf entrance since 1899 sits the magnificently restored Bond Store, now the ❼ **Museum of Wellington City & Sea**. Another Clere design, this was both bond store and head office for the once-influential Wellington Harbour Board. It is certainly well worth an extended visit.

Return to the waterfront past the Events Centre, venue for concerts, trade shows, sports fixtures and Olympic Museum. Call in to see a reconstruction of Plimmer's Ark near Shed 6, then continue your stroll southwards past the long expanse of Shed 6 and out to the delightful open space of ❽ **Frank Kitts Park**. This area was the last of Wellington's major reclamations and, when no longer required for wharves and warehouses, was one of the first areas developed into a dedicated public space that now brings people in droves to enjoy outdoor theatre, cultural events or just the simple ambience of this waterfront space. Right on the waterfront look for the Water Whirler, a posthumously realised work by New Zealand film maker and kinetic sculptor Len Lye. During the evenings, weather permitting, it

MUSEUM OF WELLINGTON CITY & SEA

Open daily 10 am–5 pm (except Christmas Day). This museum brings alive the era when Queens Wharf was the hub of Wellington's port activity, and features much more about Wellington's history. Entry free.

NEW ZEALAND ACADEMY OF FINE ARTS

Hours variable, depending on exhibitions. This Queens Wharf gallery holds regular free exhibitions supporting living artists.

'performs' its amazing water whirling designs on the hour.

The **❾ lagoon** comes next; it's a picturesque spot, its waters often rippled by rowing skiffs, dragon boats or kayaks. The two rowing clubs that grace the lagoon's shoreline – the Boatshed (built in 1885 and since moved twice) and Wellington Rowing Club (built in 1894 as a naval volunteer base during the 'Russian Scare') are also popular reception venues.

Continuing beside the harbour's edge, the walk crosses a footbridge, a steel crane boom construction completed in 2000 and designed by well-known Wellington architect Ian Athfield. The bridge and nearby landscaping are the early stages of waterfront development that has been the subject of much public debate.

The bridge leads onto **❿ Taranaki Wharf**. Look out for the maritime relics – buoys, anchors and giant shipping chains – displayed on the island near the bridge. Look, too, for the bronze Kupe statue, which found a permanent home here in 2000 after several moves around the city over a 60-year period. Sculptor William Trethewey designed the neoclassical statue for the 1940 New Zealand Centennial Exhibition.

WHEELS ON THE WATERFRONT
On a still, sunny weekend you won't be walking alone along here (or along most of the waterfront for that matter) as inline skaters, 'skaties' (skateboarders) and cyclists will whisk by. The wheel brigade will likely be joined by pram- or buggy-pushing parents, and the unusual Crocodile Quadricycles will add to the colourful conglomeration.

Usually berthed at Taranaki Wharf is the *Hikitia*, the only operational steam-driven, self-propelled, floating crane in the southern hemisphere. The *Hikitia* worked at the Port of Wellington from 1926 until 1985. Private owners have since restored the crane, which can lift up to 80 tonnes.

Your walk swings left beside the water with Macs' Brewery and the Circa Theatre on your right. Looming large beside the Circa is the great

MUSEUM OF NEW ZEALAND TE PAPA TONGAREWA
Open daily (except Christmas Day) 10 am–6 pm, late nights Thursdays (9 pm)
This really should be treated as an outing in its own right. There is no entry charge, although you will have to pay for some exhibits.

> **WELLINGTON WRITERS WALK**
>
> As you wend your way between Frank Kitts Park and Chaffers Marina take time for some literary pauses. Look for the inscribed plaques of the Wellington Writers Walk, a celebration of the city's wealth of prominent writers, and of the city itself. Ponder the words of Katherine Mansfield, James K. Baxter, Patricia Grace, Bill Manhire and other luminaries.

edifice of ⓫ **Museum of New Zealand Te Papa Tongarewa**, opened in 1998 and visited by two million people within the first seven months. As you walk between the museum and the harbour you can study the big, bold statement of Auckland architect Ivan Mercep, and pass beside the contrasting green profusion of the museum's Bush City, where many of New Zealand's natural vegetation sequences have been recreated.

Yet another change of scene comes as you leave Te Papa and walk between the yachts and launches moored in sheltered Chaffers Marina, and the restaurants, ice cream bars, cafés and apartments of ⓬ **Chaffers Dock**, Chaffers being Wellington's first harbourmaster. Chaffers Dock is the stylish transformation of the former Herd Street Post and Telegraph Office. It stands island-like between the waterfront and wetlands and water features of ⓭ **Waitangi Park**. Another recent city development, completed in 2006, Waitangi Park also features extensive open grassy areas, trees and a skate park and children's playground. While controversy raged over its design and cost, the park is certainly an improvement on previous uses of this land, which included a massive incinerator plant.

WHY GO TO THE RIVIERA?

Detour to explore Waitangi Park, if you wish, then continue beside the harbour, staying by the water and walking right around the 'Overseas Terminal' wharf, where the kahawai might be running for the ever-present wharf fishing fraternity, or cutting directly across to the next marina in ⓮ **Clyde Quay**, nestled alongside Oriental Bay. The scene here is essential Wellington: marina in the foreground, quaint boat sheds, wooden villas on the hillside behind and, dominating the skyline on one of Wellington's prime pieces of real estate, the Gothic-style monastery built for the Redemptionist Brothers in 1932. The scene brings to mind an

Evelyn Page oil on canvas depiction of Oriental Bay, aptly named *Why go to the Riviera?*

The last few hundred metres of the walk explore the start of Oriental Bay. Follow the footpath above the boat sheds (built in about 1905), past the cafés, old villas and new apartments, to the **⓯ Freyberg Pool and Fitness Centre**. Beyond the pool is a carpark, playground, changing rooms and beach (with its barged-in sand), a popular spot for an eclectic mix of people likely to include families with young children, courting couples, marathon swimmers in training and outrigger canoeists.

Across the bay the old band rotunda juts out to sea. It was built in 1935 and now houses a restaurant. The bands play no more, but the Oriental Bay fountain plays its own form of music. And beyond, ships, ferries, tugboats, fishing trawlers, yachts and kayaks will be going about their watery ways.

Look, too, for dolphins, which regularly make an appearance all around this waterfront.

To get back to the start of the walk, you can double the length of the journey by retracing your steps around the waterfront (take a breather first at the café or restaurant of your choice) or pick up a city-bound bus on the inland side of Oriental Bay.

REFRESHMENTS

A plethora of dining opportunities beckons all along Wellington's waterfront, from fine dining, to casual bistro or Asian-style meals, to a brewery restaurant, to espresso, ice cream and gelato bars. Take your pick.

MOLESWORTH TO MULGRAVE
The seat of government

Government, history and architecture are the themes of this walk. Throughout the city's development architects have tried to design buildings fit for the country's centre of government. That they have achieved this, albeit with dramatically differing and sometimes contentious styles as trends, technologies and building materials have changed, is without debate.

Whether these architectural legacies are attractive or even practical is a matter of individual opinion. On this walk you can judge for yourself as you wander among some of New Zealand's grandest buildings, among the first European structures built in this country. Many have been treated with the respect they deserve: restored and maintained in their initial splendour and strengthened to withstand significant earthquakes. They are also functional buildings that serve vital roles in the day-to-day affairs of New Zealand. Most are open to public use and visitation.

For further reading, the *Thorndon Heritage Trail* brochure is available from Wellington City Council visitor centres

START/FINISH
Cnr Lambton Quay and Bowen Street

DISTANCE/TIME
1.2 km, 1 hour

ACCESS
This is in the middle of downtown Wellington and accessible via all major bus routes. The railway station is one block from the walk. You'll have to pay for carparking.

WHAT TO EXPECT UNDERFOOT City footpaths, gentle slopes
DOGS Prohibited 8 am–6 pm daily

MOLESWORTH TO MULGRAVE 25

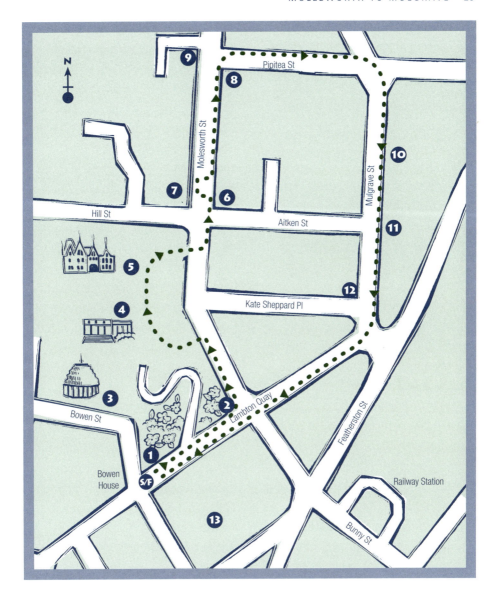

WALK KEY

❶ Wellington Cenotaph ❷ Wai-titi Landing ❸ The Beehive
❹ Parliament House ❺ Parliamentary Library ❻ National Library
❼ Wellington Cathedral of St Paul's ❽ Sir Keith Holyoake statue
❾ Magyar Millenium Park ❿ Old St Paul's ⓫ Archives New Zealand
⓬ Thistle Inn ⓭ Government Buildings

and excellent information pamphlets are available from parliament's Visitor Services. Try also the visitor centre in the Wellington Cathedral of St Paul's for books about the cathedral's history and architecture.

THE WALK

Begin on the corner of Bowen Street and Lambton Quay, on the south-western corner of parliament grounds, where the juxtaposition of old and new, in architectural terms, is immediately obvious. Directly across Bowen Street is Bowen House, the orange-brown high-rise tower designed in 1990 by architects Warren and Mahoney to house an overflow of MPs from Parliament Buildings. A walkway beneath Bowen Street allows discreet access to and from Parliament.

In contrast, 70 metres up Bowen Street is the quaint Queen Anne/Scottish Baronial-style Turnbull House. It was built in 1916 for Alexander Turnbull, a merchant who gathered a priceless collection of over 55,000 books, now regarded as one of the finest in the South Pacific. Turnbull bequeathed his collection to the people of New Zealand and it was later transferred to the National Library. In 1995 Turnbull House was restored by the Department of Conservation and is now used as a function centre.

Beside you is the ❶ **Wellington Cenotaph**, an imposing monument topped by a bronze figure on horseback entitled *The Will to Peace* by sculptor R.O. Gross. The cenotaph was built in 1929 to commemorate New Zealanders who died in World War I, then rededicated in 1952 to include those who perished in World War II. Inside is the tomb of the unknown soldier.

From the cenotaph, walk along the Quay to the corner of Molesworth Street, where two pou whenua (tribal boundary markers) mark the site of ❷ **Wai-titi Landing**, the original shoreline and for many years a landing place for waka (canoes). This was a major access point from the harbour to neighbouring pa (village sites) Pipitea and Kumutoto. The Wellington Tenths Trust gifted the pou whenua to the City of Wellington on behalf of Te Atiawa/Taranaki people, to recognise the significance of the site. During the 1840s Wellington's first tavern was located here, patronised mainly by whalers. The plantings here are mainly pingao, a native sand-binding plant prized by Maori weavers.

Walk around the corner into Molesworth Street and, on the left, enter a gateway into parliament grounds, where you will possibly be joined by protesters or petitioners, though more likely by city workers and civil servants scurrying through on a short cut. Perhaps the red carpet will be trailing down parliament steps, awaiting the footfalls of a visiting dignitary or state leader.

The grounds are a treat, an oasis of sorts. The landscaping ensures that large groups of people have space to assemble and that the buildings are not hidden from view. The mainly native plantings include pohutukawa trees, which do not naturally grow so far south, but during summer – especially when they are ablaze with red flowers – who cares!

Two 19th-century prime ministers, John Ballance and Richard John Seddon, are immortalised as statues within the grounds, and outside the Beehive there is a plaque commemorating the bicentenary of the arrival in New Zealand of Captain James Cook.

❸ **The Beehive** is the obvious name for what is formally known as parliament's executive wing. Designed by English architect Sir Basil Spence, since its completion in 1982 it has housed cabinet ministers and the prime minister – and attracted considerable comment, not all complimentary, as to its rather distinctive design.

AFFAIRS OF STATE
Beside the Beehive, the Edwardian neoclassical building of ❹ **Parliament House** stands in stately contrast. Its grand façade features Coromandel granite and Takaka marble. Designed by John Campbell, this building was constructed as a replacement for the first Parliament House, which burnt down in 1907. It was originally designed to be twice the size but a second wing, planned for the site where the Beehive now stands, never eventuated.

During the 1990s Parliament House underwent an extensive restoration, which included the remarkable feat of installing rubber 'isolators' beneath the entire building as an earthquake safeguard. The building is now reputed to be capable

PARLIAMENT TOURS

Tours last one hour and run daily Phone 0-4-471 9999 or visit www.parliament.nz/en-NZ/Visiting/Tours Excellent guided tours of Parliament House and the Parliamentary Library are offered, free of charge, by parliament's visitor services. There is also a visitor centre with gift shop in the ground-floor foyer.

of withstanding an earthquake to the magnitude of 7.5 on the Richter scale. A look at this technology is included as part of a most interesting parliament tour.

Moving along . . . beside Parliament House stands the Victorian Gothic style ❺ **Parliamentary Library**. Designed by Thomas Turnbull and built in 1899, it survived the 1907 fire that destroyed the original Parliament House, but the library was refurbished to its original style after being extensively damaged in a fire in 1992. A visit to the stunning foyer of this building is also included in the parliament tour.

In front of the library, take time to smell the roses. The impressive rose garden here is bordered by a Womens' Suffrage memorial, built in 1993 to commemorate the centenary of New Zealand becoming the first country to give women the vote. Also growing here are several white-flowering 'Kate Sheppard' camellias, named after Kate Sheppard who spearheaded the women's suffrage movement in New Zealand. Kate Sheppard also features in both the street name and apartments directly opposite Parliament House.

The theme of politics continues in the Backbencher pub, on the corner of Molesworth Street and Kate Sheppard Place, where satirical puppets of politicians and a menu of meals named

> **WELLINGTON CATHEDRAL**
> Visitor centre open weekdays 9.30 am–4 pm, Saturdays 10 am–4 pm, Sundays variable. Phone 0-4-472 0286 or visit www.cathedral.wellington.net.nz Guided tours are available on request, bookings required. The cathedral hosts regular lunchtime recital series.

after current MPs are entertaining features. Across Kate Sheppard Place is one of this area's modern buildings, the High Court. It was opened in 1993 and features several specially commissioned New Zealand artworks.

Continue up Molesworth Street (which, like Lambton Quay, was named for a supporter of the New Zealand Company). Pass the Court of Appeal and cross Aitken Street to the formidable concrete edifice of the ❻ **National Library**. This immense library holds national collections of research material, including the largest collection of printed Maori material in the world. It also houses the Alexander Turnbull Library. The library is closed until 2012 for building redevelopment; its contents relocated to several temporary locations around the city.

SPIRITUAL CENTRE

By now you will have undoubtedly noticed, across Molesworth Street from the National Library, New Zealand's largest cathedral, the ❼ **Wellington Cathedral of St Paul's**. The wish of Wellington's Archbishop Owen, expressed in 1958, that 'Every nation needs in its capital city a great church to express its belief in the things of the spirit' was truly realised with the creation of this most impressive spiritual centre.

After 39 long years of design and building, the cathedral was finished in 1998. Designer Cecil Wood died before building had even begun – it was finally completed under the guidance of Sir Miles Warren, who endeavoured to stay as faithful as possible to Wood's original concept.

The cathedral is a venue for many state and civic occasions, music performances and art exhibitions. Among its special features are a large four-manual pipe organ, etched and stained glass, and a historic wooden chapel.

Continue along Molesworth Street, cross to the Molesworth Arcade and look for the ❽ **Sir Keith Holyoake**

> **OLD ST PAUL'S**
> Open to visitors daily 10 am–5 pm (except during private services).
> Phone 0-4-473 6722 or you can visit www.oldstpauls.co.nz
> Volunteer guides will answer questions and there is an information display and souvenir shop. Donations are welcomed.
> There is also a regular programme of lunchtime and evening concerts.

statue in the courtyard. Holyoake, prime minister for 13 years and governor-general for a term, walked regularly past this spot on his way to parliament from his home at 41 Pipitea Street.

On the corner diagonally opposite, the carved gateway and garden denotes the ❾ **Magyar Millennium Park**, a memorial to the Hungarian population of New Zealand.

Turn onto Pipitea Street, which is named for the Maori village that was once located on the waterfront near here. Today's Pipitea Marae, on Thorndon Quay, is an urban marae that is open to people from all tribes.

Approaching the Pipitea/Mulgrave Street corner you will note a significant Pacific peoples' flavour. Housed in what were originally residential homes you will come across first the High Commission of Fiji, while across Mulgrave Street is the Cook Islands High Commission. The jumble of buildings diagonally across this intersection make up Wellington Girls College. One of Wellington's oldest schools, it was founded in 1883 and has occupied this site for all but its first few years.

Turn right into Mulgrave Street and look across the road for ❿ **Old St Paul's**, the magnificent English Gothic church that nestles behind several impressive pohutukawa trees. The church was built in 1865 with kauri, rimu and totara timbers; its architect was clergyman Frederick Thatcher and it is regarded today as one of New Zealand's finest examples of early architecture. Old St Paul's was Wellington's cathedral until 1964 and it is now administered by the New Zealand Historic Places Trust. Regular concerts take advantage of the cathedral's splendid acoustics.

HOUSE OF KNOWLEDGE

Next door to the church is Bishopscourt, built almost entirely of heart totara for the Anglican Bishop Hadfield. Next door again is a rather more modern affair, the ⓫ **Archives New Zealand**. Te Whare Wananga, the House of Knowledge, holds government records from the beginning of British government in New Zealand. The archives also hold the Treaty of Waitangi, which is displayed along with many other significant documents in the public Constitution Room. There are also regular, changing exhibitions and artworks to admire; such as a Rangi Hetet carving and Fred Graham's *Four Winds and Seven Seas* work.

Continue down Mulgrave Street, looking directly ahead to the great brick edifice of the Wellington railway station, to the historic ⓬ **Thistle Inn**, which has been dispensing ale from this site since 1840 when it sat right on the beachfront. The Inn was rebuilt in 1866, and restored in 2006. Call in for an ale and to peruse the historic photos on display.

Cross Kate Sheppard Place and walk along the northern end of Lambton Quay first beside the bus terminal, then the Pipitea Campus of the Victoria University of Wellington, to return almost to the starting point

ARCHIVES NEW ZEALAND

The Reading Room, Treaty of Waitangi and exhibition galleries are open to the public weekdays from 9 am–5 pm. Phone 0-4-499 5595 or visit www.archives.govt.nz

of this circuit. Now is your chance to visit the second-largest wooden building in the world, the grand old ⓭ **Old Government Buildings**.

Built on newly reclaimed land in the 1870s, Old Government Buildings once housed the entire civil service (which now fills several high rise office towers all around this very government department-focused end of the city). Though built of kauri, the building is designed to resemble an Italian stone palace. In 1996 the Department of Conservation completed extensive restoration and strengthening work. The building now houses the Victoria University Law School. Historic displays and some of the magnificent interior architecture, such as the grand sweeping staircase, are accessible to the public six days a week. A lone kauri tree grows by the main entrance, undoubtedly safe from the fate of becoming construction timber.

Having completed your tour of Old Government Buildings, cross Lambton Quay to return to your starting point at the cenotaph.

> **OLD GOVERNMENT BUILDINGS**
>
> Open to visitors Monday to Friday 9 am–5 pm. Visitors can view historical displays and interpretation rooms on the ground floor, and the Cabinet Room on the first floor. Guided tours are offered on occasions, phone Department of Conservation visitor centre 04 384 7770.

CIVIC SQUARE TO COURTENAY PLACE

Civic pride in the café capital

The changing face of Wellington city is nowhere more evident than in this little circuit of civic buildings, malls, theatres, restaurants and carefully landscaped open spaces. There have been dramatic physical changes. Much of this walk was once swampy lagoon or under water, until earth movements and reclamation raised the land level. There have also been changes in the people who have lived and worked here – from the Taranaki tribes that occupied Te Aro kainga (village) during the 1800s, to the eclectic mix of people thronging the city streets today. These include suited office workers around Civic Square, visiting conference delegates 'networking' around Wellington Convention Centre, a vibrant mix of cultures in Cuba Mall, and theatre buffs and party folk who emerge at night in the Courtenay Place entertainment precinct.

For further reading, check the Heritage Trail

START
Jervois Quay, by Civic Square

FINISH
Cambridge Terrace/Courtenay Place

DISTANCE/TIME
1 km, 40 mins (one-way)

ACCESS
Most Wellington buses pass several stops on this walk. The railway station is 10 minutes' walk from the start and, if you must take a car, you'll need to pay for parking.

WHAT TO EXPECT UNDERFOOT City footpaths, no hills
DOGS Prohibited 8 am–6 pm daily

brochures *Te Aro, Old Shoreline* and *Te Ara o nga Tupuna* (The path of our ancestors).

THE WALK
We start amid the artworks and interesting spaces of the ❶ **City to Sea bridge** that links Jervois Quay, on Wellington's waterfront, with Civic

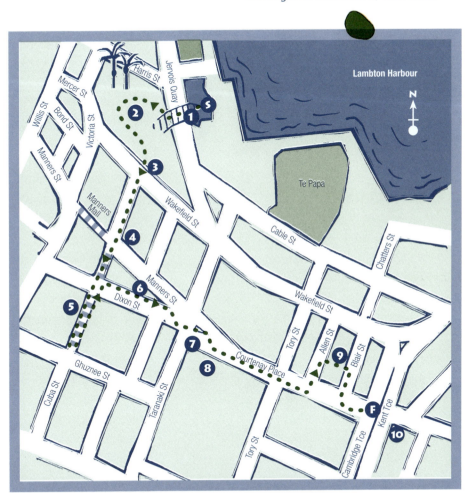

WALK KEY

❶ City to Sea bridge ❷ Civic Square ❸ Michael Fowler Centre
❹ James Smith Corner ❺ Cuba Mall ❻ Te Aro Park
❼ Courtenay Place Park ❽ St James Theatre
❾ Exchange Atrium ❿ Embassy Theatre

Square. This is much more than a bridge, with places to sit, the harbour outlook to admire and artworks and sculptures to ponder.

Artist Para Matchitt has placed gateway poles, whales and birds, and celestial representations across the bridge to reflect the link between the city and the sea as well as the arrivals of Maori and Europeans. '... This is the city of action, the world headquarters of the verb', writes Lauris Edmond on a Wellington Writers Walk plaque. Lining the steps from the bridge into ❷ **Civic Square** are two Matt Pine sculptures, entitled *Capital* and *Prow*. In the square a Ralph Hotere and Bill Culbert work graces the entire façade of the City Gallery. It's called *Faultline* and, as with all of these artworks, there is a plaque to explain its meaning. Beside the Town Hall *Anchor Stone*, by Ra Vincent, commemorates Wellington's centenary.

Civic Square was transformed in the early 1990s, when these artists were commissioned and Wellington architect Ian Athfield employed to instil a New Zealand identity, to set this group of buildings apart from other civic squares around the world. The result? Bringing together a disparate group of buildings, each quite stunning in its own right, adding sculptures and Athfield's famous copper nikau palms – well, you can judge for yourself.

The classical-style City Gallery was built in 1939 as the public library. The adjacent new library was

CITY GALLERY

Civic Square
Open daily 10 am–5 pm
Visit www.citygallery.org.nz
Free entry except for major international exhibitions.
This gallery has a reputation for innovative exhibitions of art, architecture and design. New Zealand artists and major international figures exhibit in this landmark building in Civic Square.

CAPITAL E

Civic Square
Visit www.capitale.org.nz
Admission varies.
A unique venue that presents theatre, exhibitions and events for families, including the McKenzie Theatre, interactive shows and a 'hands-on' toy shop.

completed in 1992 and Mercer Street, which ran between the library and town hall, was closed to create Civic Square. Across the square is the grand Town Hall, its design described as neo-mannerist/classical, a typical style for Victorian municipal architecture. When it was built in 1904, the building's auditorium was regarded as one of the top 10 in the world. Today the old building is part of the Wellington Convention Centre, along with the distinctly different ❸ **Michael Fowler Centre**, which was designed by architect and former Wellington mayor Sir Michael Fowler.

CIVIC SQUARE TO CITY MALL

Walk the lane between the Town Hall and the Michael Fowler Centre, cross Wakefield Street to Cuba Street and continue, past shops and inner city apartments, to Manners Mall, on what is known as the ❹ **James Smith Corner**. The Art Deco-style James Smith building was established by a city retailer, James Smith, in 1907, and was a major department store until its closure in 1993. The building is now used as a market. Across Cuba Street is another grand old building, the classical-style former BNZ, built in 1913 and now proving extremely popular as a fast food outlet. The Renaissance Apartments since added atop the former bank have earned architectural awards for their design, in keeping with the classical style.

Now for ❺ **Cuba Mall**, the first city mall developed in New Zealand and undoubtedly the only street with such an atmosphere. The sign at the mall entrance sums it up: beneath a sculpture described in a local paper as a 'jarring explosion in aluminium' is an alphabetical list of what Cuba Mall offers that runs from A to V – it doesn't get quite to Z. Wander through the mall, take in the cacophony of cultures, colour and sound – where music stores compete with busking saxophonists, singers, drummers and dancers and the constant clunking and splashing of the mall's absolutely unique bucket fountain.

There are heritage buildings too, for this is Wellington's earliest retail region. These buildings are well described in the *Te Aro Heritage Trail* brochure. Once you've had your fill, turn into Dixon Street and walk towards Courtenay Place, on the way passing through ❻ **Te Aro Park**, more commonly referred to as Pigeon Park, for obvious reasons. Across the road is the Opera House, an Edwardian theatre built in 1912, restored in 1977 and the venue still for major theatrical shows.

SWAMPS AND SHELLFISH

Te Aro Park is the site of the former Te Aro kainga, where Te Atiawa people lived in the 1800s and fished for shellfish and eels from the surrounding swamps and mudflats. The village is remembered in the landscaping and designs created by Maori contemporary artist Shona Rapira Davies in a project that took two years and more than 20,000 handmade tiles to complete. In the work the 'female principle' is represented by the pools and seating areas, and the 'male principle' by the prow of a waka (canoe) at the eastern end of the park.

Walk to the prow, cross Manners Street then Taranaki Street, turn left and walk 50 metres along Taranaki Street to the glass-fronted Te Aro Pa visitors' centre. The centre contains the preserved foundations of two whare ponga (buildings made with tree fern), remains from Te Aro Pa uncovered during construction of a new apartment building. Interpretation signs describe the site's history and how its been preserved. Public entry is free, 9 am–5 pm daily.

Return to and cross Courtenay Place to **❼ Courtenay Place Park**, with its marble sculpture *Te Moana* (The Sea) and heritage listed (now closed) underground pubic toilets. Continue along the south side of Courtenay Place and you will come to the **❽ St James Theatre**, one of the great restoration stories of Wellington.

When the original theatre was built in 1912, with a grand classical façade and magnificent interior, it was considered one of the finest architectural designs of its kind in Australasia. However, during the heady days of sharemarket speculation in the 1980s, this and neighbouring buildings were tagged for demolition. Then the stockmarket crashed and the city council, driven by public support and a private trust, set about restoring the theatre. The restored St James, which reopened in 1998, is three times its original size and includes several function areas and a café and bar called by the theatre's affectionate nickname, the Jimmy.

Two doors along stands another heritage building saved from demolition by the stockmarket crash. What is now Shooters bar and music venue started out as the Beehive Bottling Company, brewing Speights beer for Wellington. A consortium of businessmen restored the grand, multi-level building, maintaining its native timber flooring, original see-through door elevator and atrium.

Cross the road towards the neoclassical National Bank building, cross Tory Street and continue along the other side of Courtenay Place, looking across at the grand frontage of the Paramount Theatre, now an art house theatre, which was built in 1917.

OF RESTAURANTS AND RESTORATION

As you come to the corner of Allen Street, you enter the absolute entertainment heart of Courtenay Place. Allen and neighbouring Blair Streets are lined with what were once fruit and vegetable warehouses; the buildings (built in the early 1900s) fell into disuse and, like others in Courtenay Place, were earmarked for demolition. During the 1980s this was a most unfashionable, derelict part of town. However, a joint council and community initiative created a dramatic turnaround. A design concept for the streets and strengthening and restoration of the old warehouses has turned these precincts, with their restaurants and bars, into a colourful, exciting part of the city's entertainment quarter.

Wander halfway into Allen Street, then walk through the ❾ **Exchange Atrium**, where a few photos of the old produce markets are displayed, and exit onto Blair Street: more restaurants in vivid-coloured warehouse buildings, more paving, more night life.

Return to Courtenay Place and look across at the comparatively high-rise Adelphi Finance House. Originally Courtenay Chambers, built in 1928, the seven-storey tower stands out in this part of town, where a public meeting about the future of Courtenay Place in 1986 decreed that buildings should ideally be no higher than two storeys.

Turn left and walk the gauntlet of restaurants to Cambridge Terrace, where you will be standing beneath the home of Wellington's first professional theatre company, Downstage. Across the dual Cambridge and Kent Terrace roadways, dominating the streetscape of the lower end of Courtenay Place, is the ❿ **Embassy Theatre**. Built in 1924 and originally known as the De Luxe, the Embassy underwent major restoration in 2003 in time to stage the world première of the multi-Oscar award-winning *Lord of the Rings: Return of the King*. This was the third film in the Lord of the Rings trilogy, all shot in New Zealand under the directorship of Wellington's own

> **REFRESHMENTS**
>
> This walk enters the heart of the café capital, Wellington's bar and restaurant quarter – and not forgetting multi-cultured Cuba Street!

Peter Jackson.

To finish your tour check out one of this walk's little oddities. On the island between Kent and Cambridge Terraces is an ornate little building that started life in 1928 as one of the city's underground toilets. Traditionally known as the Taj Mahal, for its distinctive Indian style, it housed the Taj Mahal Restaurant for many years until being restored and reinvented as a bar.

This walk ends here, but do not feel stranded. You are in the entertainment centre of the city. Make the most of it! Alternatively, walk back the way you came or catch a bus to wherever you want to go. All major bus routes pass through Courtenay Place.

ZEALANDIA: THE KARORI SANCTUARY EXPERIENCE
A remarkable conservation story

START/FINISH
Waiapu Road, Karori

DISTANCE/TIME
6 km, 2-3 hours (return)

ACCESS
Waiapu Road turns to the south on the Karori side of the Karori road tunnel. The sanctuary, visitor centre and carpark are located at the end of Waiapu Road.
By bus, take any of numbers 12, 17, 18, 21, 22 and 23 from the city and alight immediately after the Karori tunnel. From here it is a 5 minute walk down Waiapu Road to the sanctuary.
Entrance to the sanctuary is through the visitor centre.

NOTE Zealandia is open every day (except Christmas Day) 10 am–5 pm (last entry 4 pm). Entry fees (subject to change) are $15 adults, $7 children, $37 family pass. No charge for preschoolers and Karori Sanctuary Trust members. Entry includes a map and information leaflet. Nocturnal tours, guided walks and boat trips are also available. For bookings and further information phone 0-4-920 2222 or visit www.visitzealandia.com
WHAT TO EXPECT UNDERFOOT Paths, sealed road and forest tracks, some to wheelchair standard
DOGS No
MOUNTAIN BIKES No

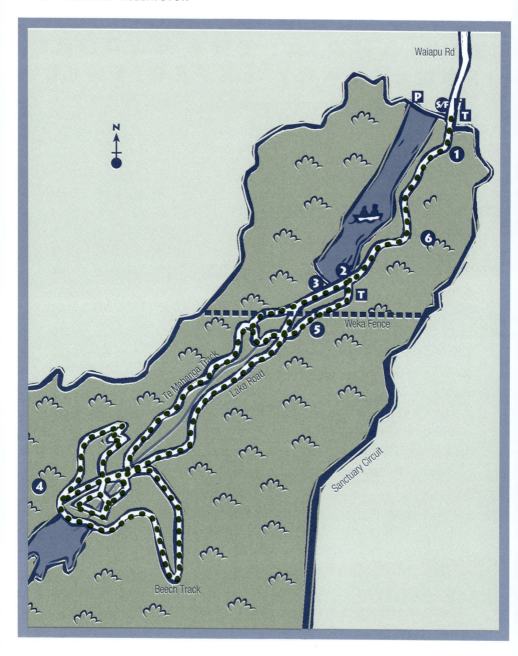

WALK KEY

1. Birdsong Gully 2. Pontoon Walkway 3. Keith Taylor Wetland
4. Viewing Tower 5. Tuatara Enclosure 6. Morning Star Mine

Karori Sanctuary is a valley of regenerating forest, just 2 kilometres from downtown Wellington, and is one of the most significant conservation projects ever undertaken in New Zealand. The 252-hectare valley lost much of its original forest through farm clearance and fire in the mid 1800s, but in 1908 it was declared a water catchment area and closed for farming and public access. In the 1990s the two reservoirs in the valley were decommissioned and the valley reopened to public access. By this time the valley's native forest had enjoyed nearly 90 uninterrupted years of regeneration.

In 1995 the community-based Karori Wildlife Sanctuary Trust took over management of the valley for the Wellington City Council. The trust set in place ambitious plans to restore the forest to its original state, create new habitats and establish a secure native wildlife sanctuary. The trust secured the backing of many community funding agencies and thousands of community members and volunteers, and has worked with the council and the Department of Conservation to pursue its aims.

A major achievement was the construction of a specially designed $2.2 million fence around the sanctuary's perimeter to keep animal predators out. Predators caught inside the fence have been eradicated, so that native birds and invertebrates can survive without threat from such pests as possums, cats, rats and stoats.

The way has thus been cleared for some of New Zealand's rarest and most endangered species to enjoy safe refuge. Native robins, weka and little spotted kiwi (the first of this species to live on the mainland in a hundred years) were the first species to be released into the valley. More ambitious releases of flying species followed, with whiteheads, saddlebacks (also restored to the mainland), bellbirds and kaka joining the avian fray. While these birds can and sometimes do fly over the sanctuary fence (and back), in general they have settled well, nesting and breeding in their new home.

Other species, including tuatara, Cook Strait giant weta and the Maud Island frog have also been released in the sanctuary.

The health and speed of native regeneration has quickly improved with the lack of foliage-browsing animals. Maturing native forest in the valley includes an abundance of tawa, kohekohe, hinau, rewarewa and pukatea trees, while lower-growing mahoe and five-finger are prolific.

Education, recreation and tourism are key components of the trust's

SANCTUARY CIRCUIT

This 9-kilometre multi-use track, known as the Roller Coaster, follows the fenceline around the sanctuary. It can be accessed from Waiapu Road, Denton Park, the Brooklyn wind turbine, Wrights Hill or Campbell Street, and offers panoramic views of the city and the sanctuary.

NOCTURNAL AND OTHER GUIDED TOURS

Here's your chance to experience the sounds and sights of New Zealand's native bush at night. The sanctuary's 2-hour night tour listens for the calls of nocturnal birds, the kiwi and morepork, passes the 'shag roost' trees and glow-worms, and if you're lucky encounters little spotted kiwi. The tours run daily, starting half an hour before sunset. Cost per head is $60 (adult), $35 (age 12 to 16) and half price for members and accompanying friends. Minimum age is 12. Bookings are essential. Several guided tours are also available by day, as well as cruises by electric boat on the lower reservoir.

plans for the sanctuary. Here's where the walks come in. After the reservoirs were decommissioned an ad hoc network of tracks was developed through the valley. The trust has refined this network and created a circuit that encompasses the best scenic, historic and native wildlife features of the sanctuary.

Walks now range from paths with grades suitable for wheelchairs to steeper and more extensive tramping tracks. Throughout the sanctuary features such as 'weta hotels', bird feeders, bird cams (which enable viewing of nests via hidden cameras), viewing hides, nesting boxes, a viewing tower and informative displays – and more – add to the experience.

THE WALK

Once inside the sanctuary, the first thing to do is explore the Charles and Mary Todd Heritage Area, which encompasses the boat shed, valve tower and bridge at the lower end of the bottom reservoir. These structures represent a special pioneering period of architectural design in New Zealand. When the dam was completed in 1874 it was the first 'modern' water supply for Wellington city and was the first concrete-built dam in Australasia. Both the valve tower, which has become a symbol of the sanctuary, and the boat shed are of neo-Gothic design, and are listed on the New Zealand Historic Places Trust register. The boat shed was reportedly built to store an early governor-general's boat by his exclusive fishing spot!

To begin your walk take the sealed road, known as Lake Road, which leads away from the entrance gate and very soon to a display explaining the making of the predator-proof fence. Soon after passing a lizard shelter (look for the rare, and very brightly coloured, Wellington green gecko), Lake Road follows alongside the lower reservoir, Roto Kawau (lake of the shag). The trail passes through an area of pine trees – much of the lower valley was planted in experimental plantations in the early to mid 1900s and the ageing pines now pose a problem for sanctuary management. Some 300 were extracted when the fence was constructed, and it is planned the remaining pines will be taken out over a 50-year period. Native species will be planted in their place. An extensive revegetation programme has already been carried out throughout the sanctuary, concentrating on plant species that provide food for native birds.

Call into ❶ **'Birdsong Gully'** to sharpen your ears to the sounds of different birds you're likely to come across in the sanctuary, then soon after the ❷ **Pontoon Walkway** and wetlands are signposted on your right. Descend the steps to the walkway which leads to the head of the lower reservoir. Here there is much to explore and enjoy: a picnic area, a 'fish ladder' that allows native fish such as banded kokopu to move from the reservoir to the wetland, a wetland information panel and the ❸ **Keith Taylor Wetland** itself, which was developed to provide habitat for native waterfowl, including rare brown teal.

Follow the track that climbs gently away from the lower reservoir to a major junction and small grassy area with toilets. Take Te Mahanga Track which gently wends its way downhill and over boardwalks along the valley floor. This involves first passing through the 'weka fence', built across the valley to separate weka from other species, for example native frogs, lizards and tuatara. Weka might eat such tasty morsels! Te Mahanga Track is also known as the start of the Kiwi Trail; signs of little spotted kiwi have been seen along here on several occasions.

The track emerges on Lake Road. Turn right, cross a bridge then soon after turn left onto the Jim and Eve Lynch Track, a little circuit that rejoins the main Lake Road track a few metres on from the bridge. It's worth the detour to see bird feeders, and several nesting boxes that show off the intricate nest-building craftwork of, for example, the grey warbler, or perhaps the more destructive nesting habits of the kaka.

The circuit leads you beneath the huge concrete structure of the upper dam, then emerges in a small clearing where many of the sanctuary's boisterous kaka population often entertain at two kaka feeders.

Supplementary feed, such as sugar water and, for kaka, more solid treats such as nuts and fruit, has been provided throughout the sanctuary while the native forest regenerates; however, recovery has been so rapid since the expulsion of browsing animal pests that the birds are increasingly favouring native fruit and flowers.

From this point there's a choice: either head directly uphill on a steepish grade for 50 metres, or wend your way along the gently graded Swamp Track, through a swamp maire grove and the largest stand of native fuchsia in Wellington, to reach the valley's upper reservoir. Here a shelter and cantilevered lookout make a worthy rest point.

VIEW FROM THE TOP

Before walking across the concrete dam an optional side-trip, involving a short (150 m) climb, mainly on sturdy steps, is to the ❹ **Viewing Tower** and upper dam construction site. Built in 2007, the tower is a replica of that used during the massive task of dam construction, when concrete was poured from a hopper attached to a cable that spanned the valley from the original tower. Historic displays and former hut sites hidden among the tangled regeneration tell more of the construction story.

The upper dam was built between 1906 and 1908, but 91 years later was considered an earthquake risk (the Wellington fault runs through the valley, alongside the upper

REFRESHMENTS

The Visitor and Education Centre (opens in April 2010) offers a café and shop, along with exhibition hall and sound and light shows. Alternatively try the Northland shops (1.5 km through the Northland road tunnel) for a great fast-food selection or Kelburn (2.5 km through the Karori road tunnel) for cafés and restaurants.

Kaiwharawhara Stream). In 1991 the dam was decommissioned, the reservoir level lowered and the valley opened up to the public.

Retrace your steps from the viewing tower and walk across the dam. The view is impressive, especially considering that downtown Wellington is just 2 kilometres away. Looking up-valley there is the forest-lined reservoir, Roto Mahanga. Tiny islands have been made to provide resting places for native waterfowl, such as scaup and brown teal, and viewing hides built.

Several tramping trails explore the upper sanctuary, above the top reservoir; however, to continue this circuit, after crossing the dam turn left then head onto Beech Track, which returns to the valley floor. (Valley View Track heads to the right here and climbs high around the side of the valley.) Partway down, Beech Track splits into two, providing either a gradual descent or a steeper option, then re-joins just before meeting Lake Road. Listen as you walk for the persistent chatter that might signify the presence of whiteheads.

Turn right onto Lake Road and head down-valley, past a grassy clearing known as Tui Terrace. Look here for the huge fallen log and history timeline, also for the 'weta hotels', then take your time as you pass the ❺ **Tuatara Enclosure** on the right. Tuatara, from Takapourewa/Stephens Island in Cook Strait, were first introduced to Karori in 2005. Look carefully: they are often seen just inside their enclosure but are superbly camouflaged.

GOLD FEVER

Gold-mining history also features on this walk. ❻ **Morning Star Mine** track is sign-posted on the right, and climbs about 100 metres to the old mine shaft, carved into the hillside. In 1857 the discovery of alluvial gold in the Kaiwharawhara Stream triggered a 15-year gold rush. The valley was studded with tents, huts and alluvial workings, but by 1872 water was considered a more precious commodity than gold and mining stopped. Gold was recovered from the valley, but never to the extent of fields in Central Otago or Coromandel. Morning Star Mine extends some 20 metres to reach a vertical shaft, and its primary use today is providing refuge for the native cave weta. A locked gate 10 metres into the tunnel is open during weekends, when a volunteer guide will escort visitors into the mine.

To return to the entrance continue back to the start of Lake Road.

OTARI-WILTON'S BUSH
A native botanical garden

A substantial stand of native forest, the largest botanical collection of native plants in New Zealand, and a wheelchair-standard canopy walkway through the tree tops are what make Otari–Wilton's Bush one of Wellington's very special places.

Tucked away in a sheltered valley, over the hill from the city and harbour yet just a short bus ride from downtown, Otari is a welcome retreat for walkers and botanists – as well as the flocks of kereru (New Zealand pigeons), tui and increasing numbers of other native birds that busily converge there to gorge themselves on seasonal smorgasbords of native fruit and flowers.

At Otari more than 80 hectares of mature and regenerating native forest sit beside several hectares of planted gardens. Here more than 1200 species of native New Zealand plants, representing most ecosystems throughout our natural wilderness and collected from as

START/FINISH
Wilton Road, Wilton

DISTANCE/TIME
5 km, about 2.5 hours (loop)

ACCESS
The entrance and carpark is on the west side of Wilton Road between Warwick and Gloucester Streets.
The number 14 Wilton bus travels from the city to the main entrance.

WHAT TO EXPECT UNDERFOOT
A combination of wide, level paths and some reasonably steep bush tracks, stepped in parts, and in a few places a touch muddy after prolonged rain.
DOGS Must be on a leash
MOUNTAIN BIKES No

far afield as the subantarctic islands and subtropical Northland, provide a botanist's delight.

A network of more than 10 kilometres of paths and tracks leads around the gardens (alpine garden, rock garden, fernery, dracophyllum garden, ponga lawn and cabbage tree lawn) and throughout the native bush. Otari's information centre, Te Marae o Tane, the canopy walkway, Troup picnic area and informative interpretation panels are features that enhance any visit to the reserve.

Otari is a scenic reserve, with management vested in the Wellington City Council. Te Marae o Tane is open daily from 9 am to 4 pm.

THE WALK

With major and minor trails heading off in many directions, Otari's complex track network can be confusing, on a first exploration at least. The circuit described here incorporates parts of most of these trails, in an attempt to cover as much of the reserve as possible. If a shorter or more easily negotiated option is preferred, the circuit can be walked in sections. All tracks are signposted at junctions.

From the carpark, take the 50-metre path to the ❶ **information centre**, past the young plantings of kauri, silver pine and totara trees. The panels inside the information centre and out on the decking cover Otari's history and natural ecology. They are well worth a read at some stage of your visit.

Walk across the 75-metre ❷ **canopy bridge**, beside the tops of tall rewarewa, hinau, karaka and titoki trees. Look down onto the crowns of flourishing tree ferns and enjoy the views of Otari's podocarp broadleaf forest that extend, through gaps in the tree tops, deep into the reserve's headwater streams. Beware – you are 18 metres off the ground here and directly on the tui and kereru flight path!

In the spring, flowering rewarewa and kowhai not only look spectacular from the bridge, they also supply food for the bird's 'canopy café', as the native fruit and flowers are described on a bridge information panel. In late summer, this 'café' serves the purple fruits of tawa and, in winter, the bright-orange fruits of kohia, New Zealand passionfruit. We are not talking cappuccino at this café.

At the far end of the bridge, walk beneath the carved waharo, or gateway, veer right and follow the wide shingle path through Otari's rock garden. After 40 metres pause at the lookout and enjoy the view into the forest heart of Otari. And while here, perhaps reflect on the vision of one of

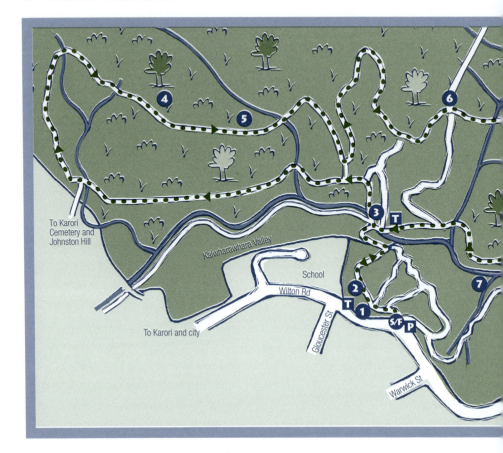

New Zealand's most eminent botanists and conservationists, Dr Leonard Cockayne, whose grave is marked by a large memorial rock beside the lookout.

LEGACY OF A BOTANIST
Around the turn of the century Cockayne worked hard to preserve what remained of New Zealand's natural habitat. Arthur's Pass National Park, Kapiti Island Nature Reserve and Trounson Kauri Park are three of the places now protected largely as a result of his lobbying efforts. But perhaps Cockayne's greatest legacy is Otari, where in 1929 he initiated a plan to establish a collection of all New Zealand's native plant species and to recreate ecosystems representative of all areas of New Zealand.

The ability to grow plants requiring differing climatic conditions has been achieved by the creation of micro-climates – the careful placement of plants on north- or south-facing slopes, for example. Such techniques

OTARI-WILTON'S BUSH   49

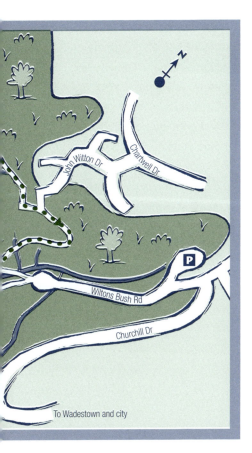

WALK KEY

1. Information centre
2. Canopy bridge
3. Troup picnic area
4. Seat
5. Giant rimu tree
6. Flax Clearing
7. Waterfall viewpoint

of mature native forest remaining in Wellington. This stand was the basis for the creation in 1906 of Otari Reserve.

From the lookout, follow the signs to 'Troup picnic area'. You descend first through planted natives and cultivars and into the shade of a small kauri grove to a junction. Otari's nature trail continues straight ahead, our circuit turns left and descends a steepish though consistently graded shingle path that zigzags down to the open, grassy 3 Troup picnic area.

This is a popular spot, framed by hillsides coloured in the rich greens of native podocarp and broadleaf forest and bounded by the pretty Kaiwharawhara Stream flowing towards the harbour. Coin-operated barbecues, picnic tables and a shelter here are well used.

continue to be used effectively by the specialist botanists and gardeners employed in Otari today.

Most of Otari is covered with naturally regenerating native forest. In 1860 Job Wilton purchased 108 acres in the Kaiwharawhara valley from Maori owners, and cleared all except 7 hectares for farmland. The abandoned farm has since regenerated into young native forest, while the rimu, tawa and hinau trees Wilton left now form one of the only fragments

INTO THE BUSH

To continue your walk, cross the picnic ground (go between the two barbecues), walk over the small bridge and, at the bush edge, pick up the trail marked with blue and yellow trail markers. From here on the walk is in the bush. Solid steps zigzag uphill for 80 metres to a track junction. Turn left. Around the corner the yellow trail veers right while the blue trail veers left and completes a 1-hour loop to meet up with the yellow trail about 150 metres uphill from this junction.

Our circuit follows the blue trail, a good, benched track that sidles southwards on a very gentle uphill gradient. The big trees here are rewarewa and karaka. Rata vines, clumps of kiekie and various ferns line the track, including the distinctive hen and chicken fern. Named for the small bulbets (chickens) which sit on the mature fronds (hens), this fern is particularly vulnerable to browsing animals such as possums.

After crossing a second little stream

KAIWHARAWHARA STREAM

A delightful 'flat walk' traverses the heart of Otari along the Kaiwharawhara Stream. It's great for those less agile. Start from the 'North Picnic Area' carpark at the northern end of Otari–Wilton's Bush, opposite the end of Blackbridge Road. A metalled track crosses a grassy clearing then enters the bush by a 'Circular Walk' sign. Follow the wide track alongside the stream, ignoring all other turn-offs, to the Troup picnic area. Cross the picnic area and pick up the Kaiwharawhara Track between the shelter and toilets; this also leads to Karori Cemetery. The track continues alongside the stream to a second, smaller open grassy picnic spot. Of interest here are the hundreds of flourishing young plants; lemonwoods, wineberries, lancewoods, flaxes and more, the result of a revegetation project undertaken largely by volunteers. Since 2000, some 25,000 native trees, shrubs and grasses have been planted along the stream.The track continues along the valley floor to Ian Galloway Park, passing a small bridge and track that climbs to Karori Cemetery, then a side-track that zigzags up about 100 m to Wilton Road, before emerging from bush and climbing 150 m around a slope to the park and rugby clubrooms. You can return the way you came, walk back along Wilton Road, or arrange a driver!

there is a junction. The track to Karori Cemetery goes straight ahead, but turn right to stay on the blue trail, which heads uphill, steeply in parts, for about 400 metres. There are some steps. A ❹ **seat** marks the top of the climb, and if you look carefully through the vegetation here you can catch tiny glimpses of Wellington Harbour.

Now the track descends, crossing two little streams (no bridges here, just hop over them) and passing through a kohekohe grove with its characteristic open forest floor. Just before the second stream is one of Otari's star attractions, a ❺ **giant rimu tree** estimated to be 800 years old. Chances are it's the oldest in the city.

Fifty metres from the rimu turn right at a T-junction. Continue descending through some open forest, past more large trees, rimu, a big old rata, and a host of fulgens rata vine thriving beside the track. At the next junction, at which you reunite with the yellow trail, turn left and follow the narrow track as it drops into the headwaters of a small tributary stream. The forest here is a delightful profusion, a typical regenerating mix of ferns, kawakawa, rangiora and hangehange shrubs growing beneath taller, light-searching rimu and rewarewa trees, whose branches are sometimes covered with perching plants and rata vines.

THE WILDERNESS OF WILTON
As the track rounds the head of the shady gully, through a tangle of vines, ferns, mosses and lichens, it's hard to believe you're just 5 kilometres from Lambton Quay. Cross a small wooden bridge, then sidle uphill around the other side of the stream to a junction. Turn left. (A right turn leads directly down to the Troup picnic area.)

Another gradual climb follows, for about 150 metres through low-growing shrubs, until a tunnel of mahoe trees leads out to an open area of grass and flaxes, appropriately known as ❻ **Flax Clearing**. It's a pleasant place to be – especially when tui are feeding on the flax flowers (late

OTARI-WILTON'S BUSH TRUST

The trust was formed in 2000 to protect, promote and enhance the unique botanical diversity and important remnant of original forest in Otari-Wilton's Bush. Public lectures and workshops relating to native plants are amongst the trust's activities. New members are welcome. Contact Otari staff or visit www.otariwiltonsbush.org.nz

summer) or surrounding rewarewa trees (early spring). Views take in parts of adjacent suburbs – Wilton, Wadestown and Chartwell – and open farmland on the ridge behind. A track heading into bush at the top of the clearing is one of many links with the Skyline Track, which follows the city's outer town belt and Skyline Ridge from Karori to Johnsonville (see page 59).

From the lower, northern end of the clearing two tracks head downwards. Both pass through similar regenerating bush. Our circuit takes the red trail (the left-hand option, facing downhill), which circles around the northern end of the reserve, in and out of a small tributary stream, through kawakawa, pittosporum and hebe shrubs, and past an exit track to the suburb of Chartwell. Turn right at this signposted exit and continue straight ahead past a second junction. The track descends reasonably steeply, passing some impressive tawa and kohekohe trees to reach one of Otari's main trails, the Circular Walk.

Turn right and follow this wide path, which meanders through the bush beside Kaiwharawhara Stream for 300 metres to the Troup picnic area. (But before you do, take a two-minute detour to the waterfall that's clearly signposted by the Kaiwharawara Stream bridge. Cross the stream, climb a few steps and turn right down the 10 metre track to the ❼ waterfall viewing platform. Retrace your steps.)

Go back to the Troup picnic area and return the way you came to the canopy walkway. Before leaving Otari, wander the Wilton Walkway to the Bushview Platform, and admire the plant collections in Otari's rock garden, fernery, dracophyllum garden, 'wild' garden and spectacular alpine garden.

REFRESHMENTS

Best options, weather permitting, are cooking a barbecue at the Troup picnic area (two free, push-button barbecues available) or carrying a picnic to the Flax Clearing. Provisions are available from the Crofton Downs supermarket and fruit shop, just 1 km along Churchill Drive, heading north towards Ngaio.

NGAIO GORGE/ TRELISSICK PARK
The greening of a shady gully

A dark, shady gully it might be to some, but take a closer look in the Ngaio Gorge and you might be pleasantly surprised. This walk meanders through groves of karaka trees and regenerating native forest alongside pretty Kaiwharawhara Stream and returns along the road where there are great views of the bush-filled gorge and Wellington Harbour.

Ngaio Gorge is essentially a conservation story, a story about a bunch of local residents who care about their backyard. For 10 years the Trelissick Park Ngaio Gorge Working Group has been a local environmental watchdog, and its members have pitched in with weed clearance and regular winter plantings of thousands of native trees and shrubs. The group has also worked with local authorities to control animal pests, weeds and stream pollution and has won several environmental awards for its efforts.

Historically, Ngaio Gorge has always been used as a transport route, first by Te Atiawa people living at Kaiwharawhara pa, at the mouth of the Kaiwharawhara Stream, then by early settlers. From the late 1800s Trelissick Track, named after Trelissick Farm at the head of the gorge, crossed the gorge from Wadestown to Ngaio. Picnics and swimming have long been popular activities in the area.

The 18-hectare Trelissick Park is managed by the Wellington City Council, and part of this walk ventures onto the council's Northern Walkway. Further historic information is available in the *Northern Heritage Trail* brochure, available from the council and Onslow Historic Centre.

Note that there are several entrances and exits to the gorge; this circuit has been chosen to provide an easy round trip and a variety of outlooks.

THE WALK

From the Trelissick Park carpark, walk down an old concrete road, lined with mature karaka trees, for 150 metres to the valley floor. This walk continues in an upstream direction, but first take a

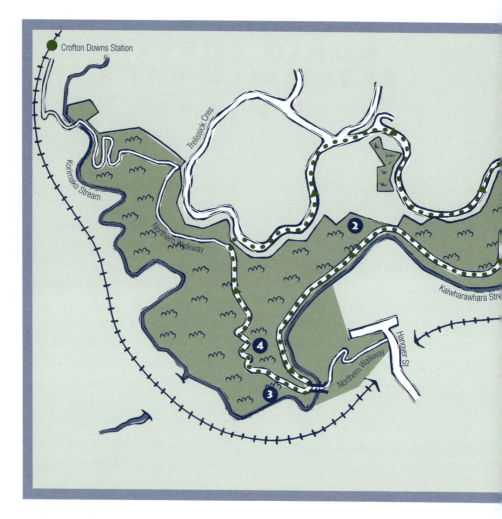

WALK KEY

❶ Kaiwharawhara powder magazine
❷ Tunnel ❸ Gorge ❹ Seat

short detour downstream.

Turn left at the bottom of the concrete road and follow the obvious track beside Kaiwharawhara Stream. Note the regenerating trees and shrubs around you; mahoe, kawakawa, koromiko, wineberry and rangiora are well represented. There is more karaka and, across the stream on the steep southern side of the gully, the bigger trees are titoki.

After about five minutes along the stream there is a large clearing, on which stands the remains of a magnificent old construction, the

NGAIO GORGE/TRELISSICK PARK 55

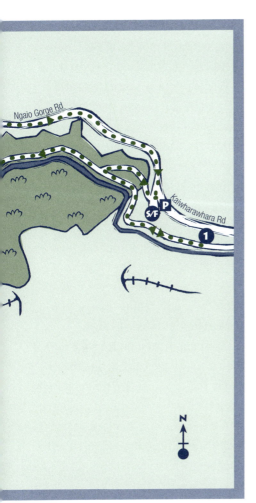

START/FINISH
Trelissick Park carpark, Ngaio Gorge

DISTANCE/TIME
2 km, 1.5 hours

ACCESS
At Kaiwharawhara, turn off Hutt Road into Kaiwharawhara Road. After 1 km, as the road becomes Ngaio Gorge Road, there is a loop road and carpark on the left. Ngaio Gorge Road is on the Khandallah bus route. By rail, take the Johnsonville line to Crofton Downs, look for the Northern Walkway track entrance off Churchill Drive, just north of the station, and walk down the track for 15 minutes to meet with this circuit.

WHAT TO EXPECT
UNDERFOOT Concrete road, metal and dirt tracks, footpath and a 15-minute climb out of the gorge.
DOGS Permitted on a leash in the gorge, but prohibited on the Northern Walkway section.
MOUNTAIN BIKES No

❶ Kaiwharawhara powder magazine. This concrete and stone building was built in 1879-80 and stored explosives when it was feared that the Russians would try to invade New Zealand. It is recognised as one of Wellington's oldest concrete structures, although it was partially destroyed by fire in 2000. At that time restoration of the building, including its original slate tile roof, was under way, but dramatically halted when a security van stolen in a robbery was hidden here and the building torched by the robbers.

Return to the bottom of the concrete road and continue now on the wide track (a council service road) which heads upstream alongside the Kaiwharawhara. The valley floor is flat here and the walking is easy.

Take time to note the native plantings flourishing on the valley floor. There's a mix of young kowhai, broadleaf, cabbage trees and flax, plus a good number of tree lucernes which are not native but are planted for good reason. Lucerne is fast-growing, nitrogen-fixing, competes well with and shades out gorse and provides good food for native birds. Native plants grow through the lucerne, which then just dies away.

Above the road and across the gully (where the Johnsonville railway line curves around a steep cutting) the steep sides of the gorge are covered with bigger trees such as titoki, tawa, mamaku tree ferns, rewarewa and ngaio. The suburb was named for the number of ngaio that grew here.

KERERU AND KARAKA TREES
Early logging operations cleared the gorge of much of its original forest and today's regeneration is a significant change from the pre-European rimu and tawa mix. Karaka is now a feature. While karaka grows naturally in Wellington; the species was also planted by early Maori for food and medicine. In recent years karaka has spread rampantly into areas where it hasn't previously grown, possibly helped by kereru spreading its seed.

The trees in the gorge are laced with plants and vines. Kohia, the New Zealand passionfruit, is tangled through the bigger tree branches, generally well hidden except during winter when its bright-orange, bird-pecked berries litter the track.

After about 10 minutes a ❷ **tunnel** looms out of the bank beside the track. This is one of two tunnel portals associated with the city's stormwater and sewerage infrastructure. Major sewer lines from surrounding suburbs pass beneath the park. Pipes run directly beneath the track in places (or form the track!) but generally are not obtrusive.

From here the track moves onto a pipeline and the gorge narrows. Tree-covered bluffs become almost tunnel-like. Just past a second tunnel the track breaks out into the open, out of the narrow gorge, and meets the Northern Walkway. This walkway follows the town belt, parks and reserves all the way from the Botanic

Gardens to Johnsonville, and crosses the upper Ngaio Gorge on its way from Wadestown to Crofton Downs. It also forms part of the Wellington link of the New Zealand-long Te Araroa (the Long Pathway).

At this junction, it is time for a short detour to a delightful, hidden spot of wilderness. From the track junction, veer left towards a small footbridge that crosses Kaiwharawhara Stream. Just before crossing the bridge, take the dirt track that continues upstream beside the Kaiwharawhara.

CLEAN AND GREEN

Follow the track for 100 metres, through a small, streamside flat shaded by mahoe trees, then when the formed track heads uphill veer left and follow the stream for a further 20 metres to an impressive little ❸ gorge. With its sheer rock walls, the stream meandering over a shingle bed and the forest-clad valley beyond, it's a wild little spot, one reminiscent of a more remote North Island forest park than a little gully in the middle of the city.

For a city stream, the Kaiwharawhara flows through an incredibly 'clean and green' catchment that includes some very special conservation areas. The stream starts high in Karori Sanctuary (see page 39) and passes through Otari-Wilton's Bush (page 46), before flowing through the gorge to its outlet in the Wellington Harbour. In the stream a recent increase in native fish numbers is evidence of water quality improvements. Eels and several galaxiid (whitebait) species – inanga, banded kokopu, giant kokopu and koaro – are known to live in the Kaiwharawhara and its bushy upper tributaries.

From this little gorge, retrace your steps to the Northern Walkway and follow the sign to 'Trelissick Crescent'. This is the only climb of the walk. It follows a wide, metalled track that zigzags out of the gorge. Take a rest on a ❹ seat partway up and enjoy the view. Steep bluffs and spurs, rock faces and ravine-like side valleys are features of the gorge.

Ignore other side-tracks (follow the posts with little orange arrows) and after about 15 minutes of climbing the Northern Walkway heads left to Crofton Downs. (This is the point to join this circuit if travelling by train.) Continue straight ahead to Trelissick Crescent and, as you leave the bush, turn right and walk 100 metres to the end of the crescent and turn right again, into Ngaio Gorge Road. Follow the footpath 1 kilometre downhill to the carpark to complete this circuit.

The Ngaio Gorge Road was first constructed back in 1845 to service Trelissick Farm at the top of the gorge.

By 1860 Cobb & Co. coaches were plying the gorge route. Across the gorge the rail link was established in 1874, and today serves as the Tranz Metro city to Johnsonville line.

The return walk along the road offers some great outlooks, to Wellington Harbour, across to the suburb of Wadestown and down into the gorge itself. Take time to look over your shoulder into the head of the gorge where steep valley sides are clothed with native forest. But best of all are the close-up views of the tree tops. The footpath passes beside upper branches of lofty titoki, tawa, karaka and rewarewa trees. Look for tangled kohia vines or, in early spring, the deep, rustic red rewarewa flowers.

REFRESHMENTS

Try the cafés in Ngaio, Crofton Downs, Khandallah or Khandallah Park.

SKYLINE TRACK
Stunning views and windy walking

This has to be one of the more uplifting walks close to the city. It is certainly one of the highest and most exposed to the weather! There are stunning views, but to enjoy them at their best you'll need to pick a good day without strong winds or cloud.

The circuit described here covers just part of the delightful walking track that traverses the entire Skyline Ridge; the farmed and forested ridgeline that overlooks the mid-western suburbs of Wellington City.

From the outset, Wellington has been blessed with an extensive town belt. Now the city is doubly blessed, with the development of its outer town belt, a long, green range of open hills that border Wellington's

START
End of Chartwell Drive, Chartwell

FINISH
Khandallah Park, Woodmancote Road

DISTANCE/TIME:
5 km, 2–2.5 hours (one-way)

ACCESS
From Churchill Drive drive 1.2 km up Chartwell Drive to the carpark by the electricity substation. Many people organise a two-car drop-off to each end of the track. Alternatively, take the Metlink Johnsonville line to Crofton Downs. The station is about 1.5 km from the mid section of the track, via Churchill Drive and Chartwell Drive.

WHAT TO EXPECT UNDERFOOT Farm roads, grass and dirt foot tracks
DOGS Yes, on a leash
MOUNTAIN BIKES Yes, except Khandallah Park. You will be able to see them coming.

WALK KEY

1. Track to Johnston's Hill and southern end of the Skyline Track
2. Skyline Ridge
3. Stile
4. Stile
5. Lookout
6. Khandallah Park

western suburbs from Karori, past Wilton, Ngaio and Khandallah, all the way through to Johnsonville. Some of these hills are farmed, a few sheltered pockets are filled with healthy regenerating native forest and some of the exposed upper slopes are covered with hardy tussock, wind-sheared native shrubs, rocky bluffs and (well, all right) a small sprinkling of gorse.

The physical bulk of these hills has forced a sudden halt to the suburban sprawl. To be on the safe side, Wellington City Council has progressively purchased land along the skyline to ensure the retention of the outer green belt and, in other areas, negotiated public access rights.

At the northern end of the hills Mt Kaukau, 445 metres high and topped with a television transmitter, has long been a city landmark, able to be seen from many parts of the Wellington region. For a number of years local residents have climbed tracks to, over and around the summit, and in 2000, following land purchases on the ridgeline south of Mt Kaukau, the council formally opened stage one of the Skyline Track, which follows the Skyline Ridge all the way from Chartwell to Johnsonville. All in all it's pretty good for a walk that can be reached within a mere 10-minute drive from downtown Wellington.

But a serious word of warning. The Skyline Track is particularly exposed. Whether the wind is a screaming northerly or a bitterly cold southerly, the ridge takes the brunt. If it's a tad breezy down in the suburbs, it's a fair bet there will be a gale howling across this walkway. The tops are also often 'clagged in' – covered in such thick cloud that visibility is zilch. It may be a suburban walk, but be warned there are times when conditions on the walkway would equal those of a mountain storm.

So pick your day, and go prepared in case of sudden weather changes. The walkway is well marked, with signs at junctions and regular yellow-topped white marker poles. Keep to the track, use gates and stiles as provided and leave gates as you find them.

The route described here starts from Chartwell Drive, climbs to Mt Kaukau and descends to Khandallah Park. There are other options, or the entire Skyline Track can be tackled in one 4–5 hour trip. However, I thought this was one of the most enjoyable circuits (not just because there's a café at the end of it!). This circuit can be tackled in either direction – starting from Khandallah Park involves a shorter but steeper climb then a long, gradual descent.

THE WALK

From the end of Chartwell Drive, go through the vehicle barrier and walk 150 metres to a gate, then follow the walkway marker posts up the farm road. As you walk look south for a great perspective of 'green Wellington': close at hand there's the bush-filled gully of Otari-Wilton's Bush, across the gully is the Tinakori Hill section of the town belt and, beyond, the forest-filled valley of Karori Sanctuary.

Continue along the farm road, which sidles gradually around the head of a valley, through old stockyards and beneath power pylons carrying their high-voltage load from Chartwell substation to the Skyline Ridge.

Small native shrubs are scattered over the farmland and grow in more dense profusion on the steeper faces. Common is tauhinu (*Cassinia*) and *Coprosma propinqua*, a divaricated shrub where the leaves grow inwards with an outer layer of twigs, thought to be a protective, anti-browser mechanism. Lone cabbage trees stand out in the gullies.

As you climb, views to the east unfold of Wellington Harbour, the Eastbourne hills and the higher Rimutaka Range. The ❶ **track** to Johnston's Hill (above Karori) and the southern section of the Skyline Track turns off to the left. Continue straight ahead and after about 20–30 minutes' walk from the start of your walk, the road reaches the ❷ **skyline**. You'll know you're there because you can see the view on the other side! In the foreground Makara Beach nestles between rolling farmland and Ohariu Bay. Beyond, across Cook Strait, sprawl the Marlborough Sounds. Arapawa Island lies across the head of the sound and, if the weather is right, you might even be able to pick out the light on the rocky outcrops called the Brothers.

Look, too, for the birds that inhabit these open hills. Skylarks, harriers and, surprisingly for a species considered threatened, native New Zealand falcon are often present. Falcon have an outstanding range of vision and the open skyline ridge makes a great launching pad for speedy and vicious hunting forays down into the suburbs, for smaller feathered victims.

Turn right (northwards) and follow the marker poles along the farm road that continues over the ridge, dropping downhill briefly then meandering upwards along the ridge crest, heading towards Mt Kaukau. As the road twists and turns new views unfold on either side. A short distance along the main ridge the farm road veers left and your route goes over a ❸ **stile** and onto a grassy track. Look carefully for white-flowering rata vine, tangled in the low-growing coprosma shrubs just beyond the stile.

Continue following marker posts as the track undulates over little hillocks on the ridge top. To the right of the main ridge there is a high point locally known as the Crows Nest. Continue past a sign that indicates 'Bells Track, 10 minutes' (this track turns off the ridge a further 10 minutes' walk from here and descends to Ngaio).

Views here are a study in contrasts, depending on which side of the ridge you look – to the west is the green expanse of Ohariu valley farmland, while down to the east the city's office towers and the port's container cranes dominate the landscape.

The route drops down a fairly steep part of the ridge for about 75 metres, where there is no obvious track, to a low point in the ridge and the junction of the Skyline Walkway and Bells Track. Bells Track originally provided access to the Ngaio Railway Station for farmers in Ohariu Valley. It had fallen into disuse and was overgrown before being reopened in 1989 by the Onslow Historical Society. Now it forms part of the Wellington link in the New Zealand-long Te Araroa (the Long Pathway). Bells Track descends for 15 minutes to the top of Awarua Street in Ngaio. (Awarua railway station is partway down the street, on the left.)

In the 1800s Awarua Street was a busy milling area; big trees were felled and milled at the site now known as Cummings Park. The name Onslow (adopted by the Historical Society, as well as the local college and kindergarten) refers to the breakaway Onslow borough, formed in 1890 by residents of Wadestown, Kaiwharawhara, Ngaio (also known as Crofton) and Khandallah in protest against a Hutt Road toll gate established by the provincial government. The Onslow borough survived until 1919.

To continue on the Skyline Walkway, follow what is now a more defined grass track climbing along the ridge crest. As you climb, even better views appear. Much of Wellington city is now spread below to the east, and the Marlborough Sounds and Tasman Sea to the west.

WILD AND WIND SHORN
Just after you climb a ❹ stile take note of the vegetation hugging the ridge crest. Even if you are walking on a calm day, it is easy to see how exposed this place is by the 'aerodynamically adapted' mats of ground-hugging shrubs that survive here. Light-green tauhinu stands slightly higher and contrasts with the twiggy-brown, stunted, divaricated coprosma and gorse, all strewn with tangled rata vines and occasional bush lawyer. Beware the sting of scattered ongaonga, or stinging nettle, lurking near the track. Its bright-green leaves are a distinctive contrast with the other vegetation.

Continue the gradual climb, through rock and tussock now as well as grass. The final 200 metres or so to Mt Kaukau is a bit of a grunt. Let the views

> ## ONSLOW HISTORICAL SOCIETY
> Onslow Historic Centre
> 86 Khandallah Road
> Open Sundays 1 pm–4 pm
> Check out Onslow Historical Society's centre for information about the development of this area.

take your mind off the climb. At the top, rest on the ❺ **lookout platform** near the television transmitter, where a plane table indicates what you can see, as well as the landmarks that are hidden by trees or hills.

Between the transmitter and lookout there is a major track junction. Follow the directions to ❻ **Khandallah Park** and Simla Crescent, taking the grassy track that heads downhill towards the harbour, to a stile 200 metres from the lookout platform.

Cross the stile and descend a wide shingle track that is lined with low-growing native trees and shrubs and scattered pine trees. After about 450 metres turn left onto the signposted Khandallah Park track.

KHANDALLAH PARK

This track is rougher and quite steep, and descends over tree roots and many steps beneath higher-growing native forest. Just after a small clearing, where the forest-framed harbour and city views are a delight, the track crosses a bridge over a small creek.

These are the headwaters of Tyler Stream, enjoying a short run through the forest of Khandallah Park before being diverted underground to reach the harbour. From the bridge the downhill grade eases considerably, and a wide track follows the stream.

This land was cleared by early European settlers for farming, but Khandallah Park was set aside as a reserve in 1909, so native regeneration has been occurring now for nearly 100 years. Mahoe trees dominate, with taller rewarewa on the higher slopes, and a dense understorey includes rangiora and kawakawa shrubs, ferns, rata vines and kiekie climbing plants.

Ignore the track that turns right and crosses the stream, heading to Simla Crescent – instead continue straight ahead for 50 metres to a sealed path, which starts beside a second bridge and leads out of the bush and onto the green, grassy clearing of Khandallah Park. This small, forest-surrounded park is popular with local residents. There are picnic tables, a children's playground and a council swimming pool open during summer free of charge. Note the native fuchsia trees conspicuous around the bush edge and in the streambed. They are distinctive for their reddish-brown, flaky bark, their delicate red flowers and, in winter, for the fact they are partly deciduous. Other, planted trees which feature here include some magnificent, mature rhododendrons.

And there is the café – the Khandallah Tearooms were originally built in 1926 and for many years sold 'ice creams, lollies and hot water to picnickers in the park'. In later years the tearooms became a residential property, until 1998 when the building was once again turned into a refreshment stop for picnickers – and walkers, of course.

If you need to return to your car at the beginning of the track you can retrace your steps if you have the energy, or walk down Woodmancote Road, turn left into Box Hill then right into Station Road. Take the train from Khandallah to Crofton Downs, which will save you about 3 kilometres of walking.

REFRESHMENTS

There are good cafés in Khandallah and Ngaio, while Café du Parc in Khandallah Park is a fine spot to linger at the end of your walk.

OLD COACH ROAD
Gently graded country heritage

START/FINISH
End of McLintock Road, Johnsonville, or end of Rifle Range Road, Ohariu Valley

DISTANCE
1.5 km, 30–45 minutes one way

ACCESS
From Johnsonville drive up Broderick Street, turn into Truscott Avenue, then right into McLintock Street and continue to the end of the street. From here a metalled track leads to Old Coach Road, which can be seen following the grassy hillside just across a small gully. The metalled track begins at the end of Carmichael Street, 50 m down hill from McLintock Street.

Alternatively, head north from Johnsonville towards Churton Park and turn onto Ironside Road which becomes Ohariu Road. After 5 km there is a cross road. Turn left and drive for about 1 km along Rifle Range Road and park before the farm gate at the road end.

WHAT TO EXPECT UNDERFOOT Well compacted surface with some grass, dirt and rock. Parts can be greasy when wet.
DOGS Yes, on a leash (this is a working farm with sheep, cattle and horses likely to be encountered).
MOUNTAIN BIKES Yes, there is plenty of room for bikers and walkers.

OLD COACH ROAD 67

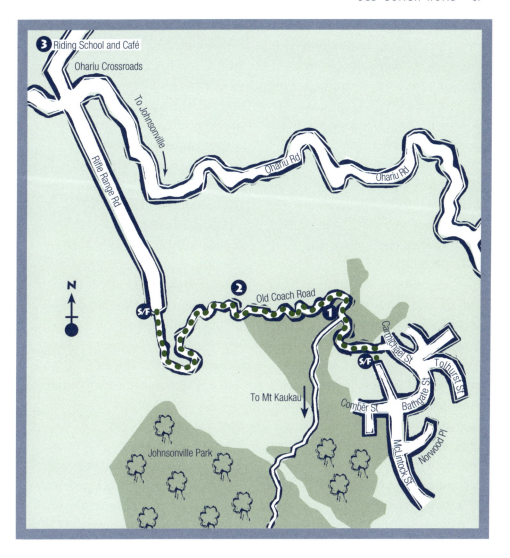

WALK KEY

1 Junction with Northern Walkway **2** Gullies with native forest
3 Saddleback Café

This is a rather short walk but its great views, rural setting close to town, a gentle grade and historic interest warrant its inclusion in this book.

The Old Coach Road has been described as one of the best remaining examples of any horse-era road in New Zealand and of an original 19th-century public works thoroughfare.

The road, originally a foot track used by local Maori into Ohariu Valley, was converted into a rough road for use by new settlers in the valley, then from 1856 to 1859 developed into the road still enjoyed by walkers and bikers today, with its consistent grade of between 1 in 12 and 1 in 15. Interestingly, this was too steep for horse-drawn coaches thus Old Coach Road is something of a misnomer. The road provided the main valley access until 1908 when Ironside Road, which leads into the valley from northern Johnsonville, was built.

In 1945 and again in 1971, parts of the old road at its Johnsonville end were widened and sealed for use by new housing sub divisions. Neglected but not forgotten, during the 1990s the road became the topic of vociferous debate between property developers, wanting to further encroach on the roadway with more housing development; the council, who sought to change the zoning from road to residential to allow such development; and a strong lobby of local folk who recognised the road's historic and cultural values. The road now has a Category One listing with the Historic Places Trust, its historic and recreational significance are formally recognised by the Wellington City Council, and it is well protected from future threats of closure.

Today, Old Coach Road is extremely popular with walkers, runners, bikers and people exercising their horses from Ohariu Valley stables. It forms the northern end of Wellington city's popular Northern Walkway and is a key link in the Wellington to Porirua section of the New Zealand-long walkway Te Araroa (the Long Pathway).

THE WALK

From the end of McLintock Road pick up the wide metal track that passes a landscaped area and rock wall. The track dips through the head of a small gully and up onto the grassy Old Coach Road, which wends gently around the hillside overlooking recent housing developments.

Cross the stile (or go through the gate provided for bikers) and soon you will see markers coming down the grassy hill on your left. This is where the ❶ **Northern Walkway** descends from Mt Kaukau and joins the Old

Coach Road, and where Te Araroa (the Long Pathway) also links up, en route from Wellington via the Northern Walkway, Old Coach Road, Spicer Forest and Colonial Knob (see page 129) to Porirua.

Continue along the very obvious Old Coach Road, following the sign to Rifle Range Road. Now you will be looking into the farms of Ohariu Valley as the road descends gently, nosing in and out of gullies and opening up views that extend, on a good day, to Cook Strait and the South Island.

Pylons are a blot on the landscape. Gentler on the eye is the native rata covering the banks and the patches of regenerating mahoe, rangiora and other native plants filling the ❷ **steep little gullies** below the road and in parts shading the road itself, providing contrast to the open farmland and shelter for the sheep.

The final part of Old Coach Road descends to the floor of the valley, which in 1911 was dammed to provide water for the then-fledgling town of Johnsonville. Water was pumped from the 70,000 gallon Ohariu Dam, just up the valley from the Old Coach Road, to a reservoir on the ridge top and from there it was piped into the town, nearly 200 metres below. However, a massive rainstorm in 1918 buried the dam, leaving Johnsonville without water. An alternative dam was built elsewhere and, later, the Ohariu Dam was temporarily restored to supplement the town's water supply until 1946, when Johnsonville was connected to the Kaitoke water supply.

The last part of this walk follows a ❸ **metal farm road** along the valley floor, beside pine and native forest and past a small farmyard, to Rifle Range Road. From here, retrace your steps to your starting point or, if you have organised transport, drive back to Johnsonville via Rifle Range Road, 1 kilometre from Ohariu Road, which is 5 km from Johnsonville.

REFRESHMENTS

There's a café very close to the outer end of the Old Coach Road; the ❹ **Saddleback Café** at the Ohariu Valley's Country Club Riding Academy, which is known for its riding school and horse-trekking adventures. Head to the crossroad at the start of Rifle Range Road and go straight across onto Ohariu Valley Road where you'll find the café 100 metres on the left. The café is open Saturday and Sunday 10 am–5 pm.

SOUTHERN WALKWAY
From harbour haven to stormy south coast

START
Oriental Bay

FINISH
Houghton Bay

DISTANCE/TIME
9 km, 3.5–4 hours (one-way)

ACCESS
The walk starts on Oriental Parade, 400 m beyond Grass Street from the city. It is clearly signposted and there is parking across the road, although spaces might be hard to find on a weekend. Buses numbers 14 and 24 travel past this entrance. Bus number 23 travels the Houghton Bay route to Courtenay Place.

WHAT TO EXPECT UNDERFOOT A wide variety, including sealed footpaths, shingle and dirt tracks, steps, grass, rocks and tree roots
DOGS Must be kept on a leash
MOUNTAIN BIKES For most of the walkway, yes

This walk extends from coast to coast, through the inner suburbs and yet stays almost entirely off road, in parks and on forest trails. Along the way, ever-changing perspectives of the city are revealed through the trees from many fine vantage points.

The Southern Walkway leaves the shelter of the inner harbour's Oriental Bay and crosses to the wild and rugged south coast along the ridgeline of hills known as Te Ranga o Hiwi (the ridge of Hiwi). Two high points are Mt Victoria, near the start, and Mt Albert, a prominent high point above Houghton Bay. Mt Victoria is a top city viewpoint and busloads of tourists visit regularly. Few tourists venture to

WALK KEY

① Lookout
② Mt Victoria lookout
③ Carillon tower
④ Mt Alfred
⑤ Wellington Harrier and Athletic Club
⑥ Truby King Park
⑦ Melrose Park
⑧ Mt Albert
⑨ National Hockey Stadium
⑩ Sinclair Park
⑪ Houghton Valley School
⑫ Lookout

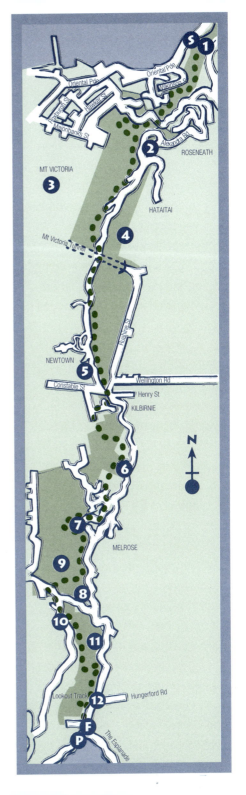

the more remote Mt Albert but the view from its summit, overlooking the south coast, harbour entrance and Kaikoura Mountains, is stunning.

The town belt concept has been a success in Wellington. More than 400 hectares of regenerating native bush, pine forests, walking and biking trails sit within the city's inner confines, a legacy of the foresight shown by the New Zealand Company when it introduced the English town belt concept here to provide space for public recreation and aesthetic values.

A confusing maze of tracks and paths with multiple entrance and exit points covers the area of the route. The walkway progresses along a bewildering mix of path, track, roadside and open clearings, and crosses roads and parks and playing fields during its 'green' journey through the city. However, it is clearly marked, and so long as you follow the walk description here and keep a careful watch for marker posts and little orange direction arrows on the trail you should stay on track.

The walkway, completed in 1979 with the help of the Wellington branch of the National Heart Foundation and upgraded in 1993, is managed by Wellington City Council.

THE WALK
From Oriental Parade the walkway starts as a concrete path that zigzags upwards beneath pohutukawa trees to reveal a quickly expanding view of the harbour and city. After about the third zigzag, detour 10 metres to a seat and a magnificent ❶ **lookout** over what is often described as one of the most picturesque harbours in the world.

As the walk emerges below a large apartment building look for a sharp right turn, indicated by an obscurely placed marker. The concrete path changes to an alternating shingle and dirt track, still heading mainly upwards but also dropping into small gullies from time to time. Pine trees, eucalypts and several natives – mahoe, karaka, cabbage trees and assorted shrubs and weeds – join the mêlée of vegetation.

About 30 minutes from the start the track crosses Palliser Road (head left a bit and look for the walkway sign across the road), then continues beneath huge, old pines. The track sidles around Mt Victoria, where there are good views up the harbour to Hutt Valley and the Tararua Range, then swings westwards where the outlook changes to one of Courtenay Place and cityscape. A long, somewhat circuitous series of switchbacks (take care to follow the walkway arrows) eventually brings you to just beneath the Mt Victoria summit.

A TANGI FOR THE TANIWHA
At this point our route detours a little from the official walkway, involving an extra 400 metres or so and a short, staunch climb to visit the summit. As the Southern Walkway continues on a gentle grade around the hillside, turn uphill on the signposted Lookout Walkway. This meets with the summit road. Walk along the road through two carparks to the road end, mingle with the tourists and climb the steps to the ❷ **Mt Victoria** lookout. The view of harbour, city, hills and mountains beyond is well worth the effort. The Maori name for Mt Victoria is Tangi-te-keo, which refers to the soul of the taniwha Whataitai. When Whataitai

was stranded by the receding tide while trying to escape the harbour, his soul left his body and flew in the shape of a bird to the top of this hill and proceeded to mourn, or tangi.

Walk back down the lookout path, pause to read the stories of former Maori occupation, and other relevant matters, on the information panels then continue directly southwards, past the memorial to Antarctic aviator and explorer Richard Byrd. At the bottom of a long, grassy slope, cross the road, walk through a vehicle barrier, beside public toilets, and continue southwards along a wide, sealed path for about 150 metres. Here a walkway sign indicates that you have rejoined the Southern Walkway. Continue heading southwards along the summit ridge.

The grassy track follows the road for some distance, offering ever-changing city vistas. To the right, the ❸ **carillon tower** stands high above surrounding buildings. Built in 1932 as a national war memorial, this is the third largest carillon in the world. It houses 74 bells, which play daily. Look out to your left and Hataitai, Evans Bay and Miramar Peninsula come into view.

As the walkway dips into a saddle, several other tracks cross at right angles. Stay on the summit ridge and follow the walkway signs to a knoll with a survey post. This is

❹ **Mt Alfred**, and directly beneath you is the Mt Victoria road tunnel. Continue through a mix of pine trees and pohutukawa, looking down to the playing fields of Wellington College, and descend a few steps to a solitary playing field. The walkway skirts halfway along the edge of this field, then veers left and leads through young plantings.

TREE PLANTING TRENDS
Fashions have changed over the years that the council has been 'caring' for the town belt. Over a 20-year period from the 1920s more than a million exotic trees, including Bishop pine, macrocarpa and eucalypts, were planted on the town belt. Now council staff, aided by volunteer groups, concentrate on planting native trees and shrubs to enhance the natural regeneration.

The walkway crosses Alexandra Road, which runs along much of the summit ridgeline. Follow the roadside for a short distance then veer left, just before the ❺ **Wellington Harrier and Athletic clubrooms**, and follow the walkway signs carefully to descend to one of the few major road intersections on the walk, the junction of Wellington and Crawford roads.

Cross Crawford Road (which heads down into Newtown), and follow the signposted walkway that leads uphill through trees to the end of Paeroa Street. Walk to the start of this short street, turn right into Colville Street, walk 100 metres then turn left into Coromandel Street. At the end of Coromandel Street climb the sealed path and steps that zigzag upwards past entrances to private homes. Follow the orange arrows carefully to avoid gate crashing! This path emerges to a service road beneath a pine plantation. Follow the walkway signs carefully through the pines, sometimes on foot tracks and otherwise on a roadway, climbing steeply in places to emerge on the rather grand driveway of ❻ **Truby King Park**.

The park, managed by Wellington City Council, is something of a hidden secret. It encompasses the Historic Places Trust-listed house built in 1923 for Plunket founder Sir Truby King, a former Karitane Hospital and extensive gardens that feature rhododendrons, azaleas and flowering cherries. The gardens are open year-round and visits to the house can be made by arrangement.

Walkway signs lead out of the park. Cross Manchester Road, then continue in the direction of ❼ **Melrose Park**, which is clearly signposted. There's a small playground at the Melrose Park sports field, as well as toilets, though these will be locked unless a game happens to be in progress.

Cross the park and look for the walkway sign at the far corner. The zoo borders the park, and you'll be able to glimpse some animal enclosures. As you leave Melrose Park the track skirts the zoo fence for about 50 metres then switches back, or you can avoid the switchback by climbing a few steps to the left, then turn left again to continue your southward trail.

From here on, expect great views. The walkway climbs, steeply at times, between eucalyptus trees and emerges at an open spot overlooking Lyall Bay and the airport. Turn right and take the lower of two tracks which soon brings you onto a wide grassy track along the summit ridge of Mt Albert.

Follow this ridge track, veering left to the airport side of Mt Albert then swinging around to the right to pass beside a water tank and the radio masts on the summit. Look carefully for track markers, they are sparse in places but they are there.

SOUTHERN HIGH POINT
❽ **Mt Albert** itself is the high point of the entire walk. Enjoy the views! Note across the valley the Berhampore golf course, which has a reputation for being one of the steepest courses in the country. On the hills beyond, the

Brooklyn wind turbine is prominent. To the east you will see the harbour entrance, Pencarrow Head and the Rimutaka Ranges. Cook Strait comes into view – with, if the weather obliges, the stunning backdrop of the Kaikoura ranges 150 kilometres away.

You are on the home straight now, as the earthen and grassy track sidles around a shrub-covered hillside where native mahoe and coprosma trees are starting to make their presence felt among the gorse and broom. Possibly you will hear the thwack of hockey sticks as you pass close to the ❾ **National Hockey Stadium**. There are other sports fields too in this area, which is known as Albert Park.

Now for the final descent. From Mt Albert the track descends to Houghton Bay Road. Cross the road, turn left and walk along the footpath, then after 100 metres turn right into Buckley Road. Walk another 100 metres, cross the street and follow the walkway signs through ❿ **Sinclair Park**. A sealed path descends a long, grassy slope, where there is a good view eastwards of the craggy Rimutaka Range, bringing the North Island's main divide to its southernmost conclusion.

The walkway continues to descend to the right of ⓫ **Houghton Valley School**, between playing fields and shrub-covered hillsides, and emerges again on Houghton Valley Road, which has by now curved its long route down into the valley. From here the walkway follows the footpath for the final kilometre to Houghton Bay.

An optional short side trip just before arriving at Houghton Bay is to climb to a grand ⓬ **lookout** above Houghton Bay Playground. Take the track signposted to Sinclair Park and Buckley Road Reserves, which zigzags uphill through regenerating bush for about 10 minutes to a view over Cook Strait and the harbour.

Once at Houghton Bay, if you have left your car at Oriental Bay, you will have to retrace your steps or take a number 23 bus to Courtenay Place, then walk or catch the bus along Oriental Parade.

REFRESHMENTS

Oriental Parade, between the start of the walk and the city, has a range of top-quality restaurants, cafés and ice-cream shops. If you venture as far as Island Bay, there is a small but interesting cultural mix of cafés and restaurants.

SOUTHERN MIRAMAR PENINSULA

A peninsula for penguins

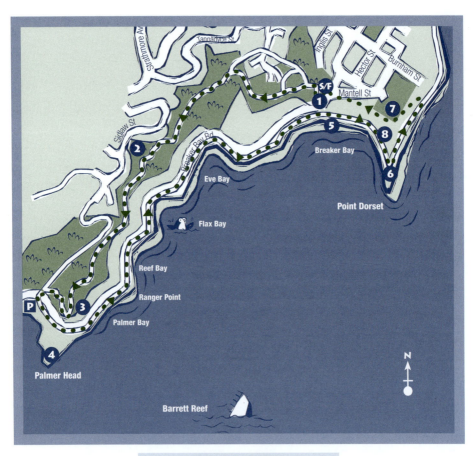

WALK KEY

1. Pass of Branda
2. Lookout
3. Ataturk Memorial
4. Wahine Memorial Park
5. Hole in the rock
6. Fort Dorset gun emplacements
7. Seatoun School
8. Fort Dorset Conservation Reserve

SOUTHERN MIRAMAR PENINSULA

This walk follows the southern crest of Miramar Peninsula from Seatoun to the south coast (along the Eastern Walkway) and returns around the Breaker Bay and Point Dorset coastline. It is very exposed. Depending on the weather, the walk may be anything from refreshing to an absolute blow-the-cobwebs away experience!

START/FINISH
Pass of Branda, Seatoun

DISTANCE/TIME
9 km, 2.5–3.5 hours (loop)

ACCESS
The Pass of Branda is on the corner where Inglis and Mantell Streets meet Breaker Bay Road.
The number 11 Seatoun bus goes to Seatoun terminal in Hector Street, 400 m from the Pass of Branda.

WHAT TO EXPECT UNDERFOOT A mix of metal and dirt foot tracks, steps, sealed footpath, grass verge and shingle beach
DOGS They must be on a leash to protect penguins, and are not permitted on Seatoun beach during daylight, November to March.
MOUNTAIN BIKES Not permitted on the Eastern Walkway

It's a delightful mixture of a walk, incorporating great views of Cook Strait and Wellington's harbour entrance, some of the region's earliest human history, more recent defence history, a touch of natural history, and some carefree beach walking and rock hopping. There are also places for reflection; a *Wahine* memorial and a Gallipoli memorial.

The peninsula landscape is a mix of housing subdivisions, scattered groves of old pine trees, and a tangled profusion of regenerating native shrubs and introduced weeds. With the help of plantings, the natives are slowly but surely overwhelming the gorse.

Fantails and waxeyes are your likely companions, shags will eye you from shoreline rocks, and gulls will be wheeling and screeching overhead. And, of course, there are korora, the little blue penguins (but you'll need to be there at dawn or dusk for the best chance of spotting them).

Local residents played a significant role during the early 1990s in forcing the closure of the Moa Point sewer outfall on the southern coast. Since then many have worked with the city council, landscaping, and revegetating the coastline, and working to protect the korora that live around the coast.

Miramar Peninsula was originally an island, known as Motu Kairanga. Whether the island was joined to the mainland by earthquake uplift, or by the stranded taniwha Whataitai, who was caught by the receding tide as he tried to escape the harbour into the open sea, can be for you to decide.

To pursue the legendary theory, when Whataitai's fellow taniwha Ngake burst from the formerly landlocked harbour, thus creating the harbour entrance, he left remnants that are now known as Tangihanga-a-Kupe (Barrett Reef) and Te Aroaro-o-Kupe (Steeple Rock), just offshore from Seatoun.

These and other names in the area refer to the Maori explorer Kupe because this was where Kupe first landed when he entered the harbour, and where he left his people to grow food and replenish supplies while he explored further afield.

More recently, Rangitane people lived on the Seatoun coast in Oruaiti pa. The small headland known today as Fort Dorset Conservation Reserve provided a fine lookout over the harbour entrance, a vantage point that was used again with the establishment in 1905 of the Fort Dorset Military Reserve. Old concrete gun emplacements remain on the headland and around the shoreline.

The high points at the southern end of the peninsula also appealed as prime defensive and vantage spots for early Maori. Ngati Tara established two pa sites on the points, as well as a heavily terraced and pallisaded pa in the valley between. These sites are now protected in the Rangitatau Historic Reserve.

MASSEY MEMORIAL

If you're still in need of memorials and harbour views after this walk, try the short, steep track at the northern end of Miramar Peninsula to the William Massey Memorial. The main track is about 200 m long, and is signposted from the roadside of the harbour edge on the city side of the peninsula. There's not much in the way of parking here, but there is at the bottom of a longer and rougher track that climbs the other side from Kau Bay.

The Wellington City Council information sheet for the Eastern Walkway, plus the *Te Ara o nga Tupuna Heritage Trail* brochure provide further information on the area's history.

THE WALK

The Eastern Walkway is clearly signposted on the inland side of the ❶ **Pass of Branda**. The start is sudden – there are 80 steps to climb – but the quick elevation provides fine views looking down onto the suburb of Seatoun, and beyond up the length of Wellington Harbour.

The track continues under some big pine trees, turns sharp left and zigzags its way to the crest of the peninsula. Ignore several side-tracks that lead to peninsula streets, simply follow the walkway signs to Tarakena Bay.

The views are impressive. Close at hand is the now deserted grassy summit of the Point Dorset headland, where guns, searchlights and anti-aircraft batteries once guarded the harbour entrance. Most impressive is the lookout onto Wellington's harbour entrance, with ships, inter-island ferries and fishing boats coming and going. Across the entrance are the two Pencarrow lights, one on Pencarrow Headland and one at shore level, and Baring Head juts out beyond. It's a good spot to reflect on the claims this harbour entrance has made on shipping. At least four ships have foundered on Barrett Reef, including the *Wanganella* in 1947 and the inter-island ferry *Wahine* in 1968.

About halfway along there is one fine vantage point looking west across to the hilly suburbs of Wellington city: Brooklyn, Roseneath and Khandallah.

The track undulates on or near the peninsula crest, at times through tunnels of native shrubbery. A tangled profusion of mahoe, broadleafs, hebes, kawakawa, rangiora and flaxes, somehow surviving constant lashings by salt-laden winds, is steadily overwhelming the introduced weeds. Just past the side-track to Sidlaw Street, take a welcome rest at the ❷ **lookout**. Look across to the peaks of Rimutaka Forest Park, the southernmost extent of the North Island's mountain divide. Listen to the waves and swells crashing on the coastline below.

The next section of track comes very close to private backyards, then descends 150 metres to meet a four-wheel-drive road. Turn left and follow this level road along the open ridge of Palmer Head. The peninsula divides into two headland ridges at this southern end, with a short gully in between. On the far, western point is the site of Rangitatau pa and, nestled below on the side of the gully, is the heavily terraced site of Poito pa. During World War II Palmer Head became the centre of coastal defence. Guns and radar were installed here to complement the fire power of Fort Dorset.

The impressive ❸ **Ataturk Memorial** sits on the eastern point of Palmer Head, where there was also once a fortified pa. It's a stunning spot with a stunning view, a fitting place to remember the thousands of Kiwi and Turkish soldiers who fought and died at Gallipoli in World War I. Mustafa Kemal Ataturk was a war general and the first president of modern Turkey.

Looking down to the sea, if the weather is calm, you may spot small boats pottering around the jagged rocks stretching out from the headland. This place is Te Kaiwhatawhata, a traditional fishing spot.

From the memorial the walk descends steeply to Breaker Bay Road, on the south coast, to the walkway exit and carpark. Our circuit continues on foot, around the coast and back to Seatoun. Cross the road, turn towards the harbour entrance and follow a grassy and sandy track for 200 metres, beneath the flax-covered cliffs of Palmer Head. This section of your walk joins the short, 1 kilometre 'Coastal Walkway', which leads from Moa Point around Tarakena Bay to ❹ *Wahine*

Memorial Park. Here a propeller from the *Wahine* rests in sight of the stretch of water where the ferry made its last, fateful voyage.

Continue walking along the coast for your return trip, past Gibraltar Rock and around Ranger Point, then along the broad, sweeping bay. Pick your way as it suits over grassy verges, boulder-fringed beaches or along the roadside, across the road from residential homes and past the signs that warn to look out for little blue penguins. Residents have built nesting boxes and planted vegetation to encourage penguins to nest on the sea side of the road, so that they might avoid dangerous crossings on their way to or from their daily fishing expeditions.

Watch for shags – black, little black and pied shags are likely to be fishing or resting on offshore rocks.

BEACHCOMBING

As the road begins its short, gentle climb to the Pass of Branda, descend the 100-metre track to the shingle beach. Why go directly back to your starting point when there is a ❺ **hole in the rock** to explore, and a rocky headland just beyond? Follow the coastline beneath the wind-lashed, flax-laden cliffs. Go through the hole, of course, then wander among the driftwood, weed and whatever else the sea has thrown ashore.

Deep shingle can make the going tough for the first 500 metres, but once around the rocky headland of Point Dorset, a roughly trampled dirt track hugs the base of the cliffs. Some of this hillside is unstable, so don't linger. Continue past the remains of the ❻ **Fort Dorset** gun emplacements. Note the thick-leaved taupata (*Coprosma repens*), a common coastal plant around Cook Strait, and the sand-binding pingao plant behind the beach, its golden hues contrasting strongly with the colourless form of introduced marram grass.

The track emerges from the rocky coastline beside the new ❼ **Seatoun School**, which opened in 2002 on the site of the former Fort Dorset. Housing developments have covered the remainder of fort land, following demolition of its military buildings in the early 2000s. Our walk turns off the beach just before the school and climbs onto the grassy, rocky ridge that leads to the Point Dorset headland, now ❽ **Fort Dorset Conservation Reserve**. This headland was also the site of the

Rangitane fortified pa, Oruaiti.

As you leave the beach, listen to the rustling sound of the waves moving the gravel on the beach – Kirikiritatangi, the Maori name for the Seatoun foreshore, refers to this sound. Two important places in Maori history here are Te Turanga o Kupe, the landing place or great standing place of Kupe, and Maraenui Flat, a cultivation area for early Maori.

Follow the rough foot track along the ridgeline onto Point Dorset, past old World War II gun batteries and observation posts, and enjoy more great harbour views. Take care along here, the track is rough and there are steep drop-offs. You are also advised to keep off the observation posts; they are old and likely to collapse. At the end of the headland the track descends directly to your starting point, the Pass of Branda.

REFRESHMENTS
There are excellent cafés in Seatoun and nearby Mirimar.

MAKARA TRACK
A walk on the wild side

START/FINISH
Makara Beach, 16 km north-west of Wellington

DISTANCE/TIME
8 km, 3–4 hours (loop)

ACCESS
From the city drive through the suburb of Karori then, 1 km past Karori's shopping centre, turn right onto Makara Road. After 5 km continue straight through Makara village, drive another 4.5 km, then turn left to Makara Beach at the Ohariu valley/Johnsonville junction. There is parking along the beachfront at the road-end. The farm section is closed for lambing between August 1 and September 30.

WHAT TO EXPECT UNDERFOOT Dirt track, grassy farm paddocks, sealed road, beach with loose rocks and shingle
DOGS No (they are only permitted, on a leash, as far as Fisherman Bay)
MOUNTAIN BIKES No

Makara Beach has long been a favourite retreat for Wellington city dwellers, be it for a beach picnic and swim on a hot summer's day, a fishing or diving expedition, or a bracing walk over the rocks when a wild northerly is lashing the coast. It's a rugged place, a rough shingle beach backed by towering cliffs where the power of the elements seems all-pervading. Though it is little more than a 20-minute drive from Wellington, there is a strong sense of remoteness about Makara.

Just a handful of people live permanently at the beach today, but in the past there have been several periods of settlement. Different Maori tribal groups have

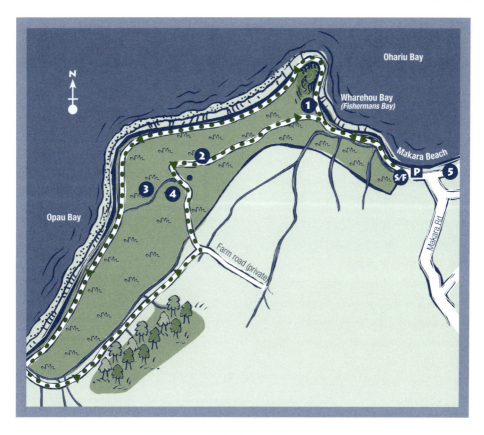

WALK KEY

❶ Boat shed ❷ Stile ❸ Gun emplacements ❹ Fort Opau Barracks
❺ Makara Foreshore Reserve

lived at Makara over the last several hundred years. During World War II the threat of Japanese invasion was guarded against by more than a hundred troops, who manned guns and radar at Fort Opau, at the top of the Makara cliffs. Later, a small Italian fishing community settled temporarily at Makara and numerous weekend baches were scattered around Ohariu and Fishermans Bays.

Much of the forest that once covered the hills has been cleared for farmland, but hardy coastal species cling to steep cliff faces or survive in sheltered gullies. Sea birds and visiting migratory shore birds frequent the Makara coast, fur seals occasionally haul out to rest, and the rock pools and bays host a multitude of shellfish, sea eggs, anemones, sponges and algae.

The Makara Track gives a taste of all the natural and historic aspects of this interesting piece of coastline. It climbs high onto the cliff tops to the old gun emplacements of Fort Opau, descends through farmland to Opau Bay, then returns along the shingle and rocky coastline back to Makara Beach.

The track has been established since 1981 and is now managed by the Department of Conservation, which also has jurisdiction over a recreation reserve and marginal strip along the coast. Please leave gates open or closed as found.

THE WALK

From the road-end at Makara Beach the walkway heads to the left (facing the sea) and follows a wide metal track around the bay, beneath steep hillsides covered with a mix of grass, gorse and matted native coastal shrubs. Before long the island wildlife sanctuaries of Mana and Kapiti (in the distance) appear beyond the northern headland.

In the bay, look for shags resting on rocks. Several species of shag – little black, black, pied and little shags – live around this coast, along with black-backed and red-billed gulls, and pied oystercatchers are likely to be foraging along the shore.

After a few hundred metres the track rounds a point and enters Wharehou or Fishermans Bay. Here is where early Maori people, possibly Ngati Tara or Ngati Ira, lived about 400 years ago and where, in more recent times, several baches were located. All that's left are the remains of an old stone ❶ **boat shed**.

Keep an eye on the water for the black, wing-like fins of the eagle rays that sometimes feed on seaweed at low tide. On the beach, common skinks and other lizard species shelter in the rocks and driftwood.

Small signs mark where the track turns away from the bay onto the farmland, just before the old boat shed. Follow the marker posts that climb a grassy/dirt track through paddocks, after 200 metres veer left and continue up a small gully, which is in fact an earthquake fault.

Be prepared for a fairly steep climb of about 40 minutes. As the track climbs there are not many marker posts, just keep following the obvious dirt track to the crest of the hill. Along the way you'll get your first glimpse of a Makara Wind Farm turbine – and depending on the wind you'll most likely hear the howling, somewhat eerie roaring of its turning blades.

COOK STRAIT FROM THE CLIFF TOPS

Continue along the fenceline on the cliff top, where the reward for your climb, weather permitting, is a magnificent vista of Cook Strait backed by the blue hills of Arapawa Island and the Marlborough Sounds. It may seem obvious, but be wary of the cliff edge!

As you continue to climb, look behind you to the Mt Kaukau radio mast and hills of the outer town belt. It is perhaps hard to imagine a major city sits just beyond those hills. As the fenceline route brings you closer to the cliff edge, the pools and rocky headlands of the Makara coast come into view far below.

The track continues on a gradual uphill grade between the fence and cliff edge, but once you reach a ❷ **stile**, your climbing on this track is complete. Take a well-earned break and look northwards to the two island sanctuaries. Other prominent points seen from here are the focus of other walks described in this book, such as Colonial Knob and the Skyline Walk.

Cross the stile and wander across the grassy headland, through little thickets of low-growing, divaricated *Coprosma propinqua* bushes, to the ❸ **gun emplacements** of Fort Opau. This would have to be one of the most stunning spots for a picnic.

On such a spot, crafted by nature's design, the old concrete gun emplacements loom with an especially ominous air, a reminder of the bleaker side of human history. There were two guns here, each with a firing range of 15 kilometres, and they were manned from 1941 to 1943. The guns were removed in 1944, without ever having been fired in anger. Today inter-island ferries, not warships, are the vessels you will most likely see from this grand vantage point over Cook Strait.

The second feature of the modern era visible from here will be several giant wind turbines, part of the Makara Wind Farm, strewn over the ridge tops nearby. In 2008 Meridian Energy began construction of 62 turbines in Project West Wind. Public access to the turbines and an interpretation centre are also on the project's plans.

From the headland the walkway leads away from the coast. Look for the marker posts leading along a farm road, past a stand of bigger native trees and shrubs in a sheltered gully, and then alongside a grassy flat where the concrete remains of the ❹ **Fort Opau** barracks still lie in the ground.

SHELTERED RESPITE

The road comes to a junction, about 100 metres from planned 'Turbine B2'. The walkway here turns right and follows an old sealed road that descends a long gully, one side lined with young pine trees, to Opau Bay. Allow 20 to 30 minutes for this downhill stretch, then follow the track as it swings towards the coast and fords the tiny, twisting Opau Stream several times. Pick your way through the huge jumble of weather-blanched logs and driftwood lying across the outlet to Opau Bay, then turn right and follow the coastline all the way back to Makara Beach.

The environment here is a contrast to the quiet shelter of the farm valley. With luck the weather will be calm, or at the very least the wind will be southerly, meaning it will be cool but heading in the same direction as you.

The terrain here may be flat but the going is far from easy, with countless water-smoothed pebbles to slip and

MAKARA FORESHORE RESERVE

Although the Makara River flows through a heavily modified farmland environment, its small estuary provides refuge for a number of wetland birds. Pied shags, white-faced herons, Caspian terns and variable oystercatchers live in the vicinity, while reef herons, South Island pied oystercatchers, royal spoonbills and white herons occasionally visit. For these migratory birds the estuary is a handy refuge where they can escape for shelter should they meet a northerly storm as they cross Cook Strait.

The foreshore reserve, established in 1999 by Wellington City Council, protects a community of native coastal plants once widespread throughout the Wellington region but now uncommon. New Zealand daphne (*Pimelea prostrata*), New Zealand ice plant (horokaka) and scabweed (*Raoulia* spp.) are three examples of the ground-hugging mat plants that grow here.

As you leave Makara, observe the native plants growing along the margins of little Makara Stream. These plantings have been established by the 'Makaracarpas', a group of local residents helped by Wellington City and Regional Councils as part of an environmental restoration plan. As well as planting and weeding, the group rallies every Saturday morning at 10am for a beach clean-up. Volunteers welcome.

slide your way over. Scrunch along nature's gauntlet between sea and steep cliffs, picking your way over and around the driftwood and detritus the sea has thrown ashore, as well as the rocks and debris discarded from the cliffs above.

As you progress towards Makara, the cliffs look a little more stable, with a thick, matted covering of tauhinu, pohuehue and *Coprosma propinqua* shrubs clinging to the steep, greywacke faces. Flaxes and little senecio plants, or groundsels, and speargrasses also survive in this harsh environment. And while on the subject of small things surviving, look closely at boulders at the base of the cliffs for little short-horned grasshoppers.

Depending on the tide and weather, as you get closer to Makara it is also possible in places to wander across exposed rocky platforms. It makes a change from the shingle beach, and gives an opportunity to look for little crabs, fish, anemones and sponges in the rock pools. Empty paua shells heaped on the beach will be a sign of someone's previous shellfish gathering; here's hoping they abided by the legal limit. Perhaps the spiky brown shells of kina (sea eggs) will also be discarded following someone's fresh feed of kai moana (seafood).

As you near Makara expect to come across people – picnicking groups, perhaps snorkellers looking for paua. Even if the weather is bad, expect to meet fellow walkers. A good storm rarely stops the staunch Wellingtonian from venturing out into the most dramatically exposed places!

If you tire of rock hopping or of forcing your way through the loose shingle, look for a vague track, more solid underfoot, that runs along the back of the beach in places. A final scramble around a rocky headland brings you back into Fishermans Bay, where the track sidles above the rocky shore and leads you back to Makara Beach to complete your circuit.

On the Makara foreshore, on the other side of the carpark from the walkway, the wetland environment of ❺ **Makara Foreshore Reserve** is well worth a look.

REFRESHMENTS

There is a café/restaurant at Makara, open Thursdays to Sundays. The nearest shops to Makara are at Karori, 12 km away. If all else fails, take that picnic to the Opau headland.

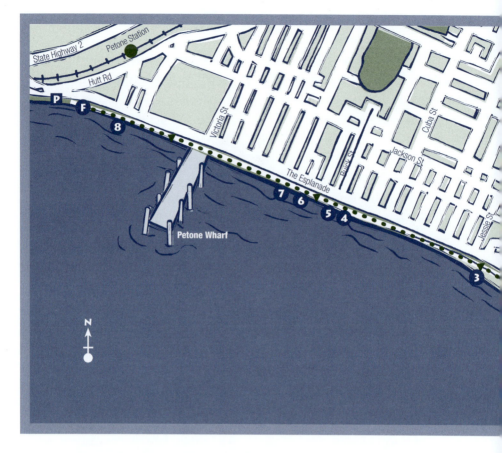

PETONE ESPLANADE
History, harbour and heaps of fun

Petone Esplanade Walkway has lots going for it: no hills, a constant harbour view, history, a playground, a model train and some delightful landscaping, artwork and coastal plantings, including some very special native plants.

This area was once a swampy flat, where harbour met wetlands and over which the Heretaunga River meandered, at times in flood, into the harbour.

A few hundred metres inland from the shore, dense forest filled the river

PETONE ESPLANADE 89

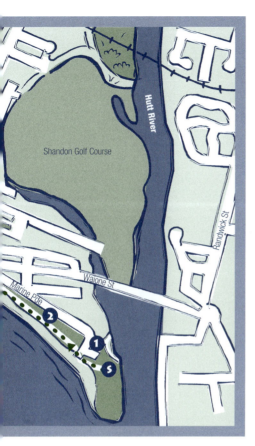

WALK KEY

1. Hikoikoi Reserve
2. McEwan Park
3. Lions Park
4. Cross of Iona
5. Petone Settlers Museum
6. One Thousand Hand Park
7. Heretaunga Boating Club
8. Korokoro Gateway

around the edge of the harbour and opened the way for the construction of a road to link the new Wellington city with the valley of the Heretaunga or Hutt, as the river came to be known.

For some years the Petone foreshore was largely ignored, neglected even. But local pride and council initiatives have turned that around. Since 1997 thoughtful planning by community groups and the council has resulted in the whole foreshore becoming a place to visit, wander, explore and enjoy. There's lots to see and do, and the flat terrain and paths are great for pushchairs and wheelchairs.

valley. In 1840 the first New Zealand Company ship anchored in the harbour, and as longboats ferried English settlers to the shore local Maori from the Pito-one pa at Korokoro ventured out in waka to greet them. Soon after, a flooded Heretaunga influenced the settlers to move to Thorndon, which became Wellington city.

Today the swamps have been drained, assisted in no small way by the massive Wellington earthquake of 1855 that uplifted several metres of land all

THE WALK

The eastern end of the Esplanade Walkway begins at **1 Hikoikoi Reserve**, beside the western bank of the Hutt River. Hikoikoi Reserve is named for the Te Atiawa pa site that was once located here.

START
Hikoikoi Reserve, Marine Parade, Petone

FINISH
Korokoro Gateway carpark

DISTANCE/TIME
3 km, 1.5 hours (one-way)

ACCESS
By car, drive to Hikoikoi Reserve carpark, at the eastern end of Marine Parade. The Eastbourne bus stops near each end of the Esplanade, by the Waione/Jessie Street junction in the east, and the TransAlta building on Hutt Road at the western end. Petone railway station is 20 minutes' walk from the Esplanade.
Wellington's East by West Ferry Harbour Explorer Tours call at the Petone Wharf three times daily during weekends and public holidays.

WHAT TO EXPECT UNDERFOOT Sealed footpaths and shingle paths. Beach walking optional.
DOGS Yes, with various restrictions. Check with Hutt City Council.
MOUNTAIN BIKES Yes

More recently the reserve, the former site of a glass factory and rubbish tip, was an industrial wasteland. A $1 million fund, which came from rents paid by industries to the former Petone Borough Council, has been put to good use landscaping the reserve. Native plantings, established in 1997, include coastal species suited to the harsh, salty environment. There are also several karaka trees planted by the Royal Forest and Bird Society and a few Norfolk pines and macrocarpa trees.

There are two large viewing platforms in the reserve, hidden among the fast-growing plantings, one overlooking the Hutt River outlet and another facing out to the harbour. This is a more 'remote', rugged end of the foreshore, where hardy taupata (*Coprosma repens*) survives on the rough shingle beach. Gulls, terns and shearwaters are likely to be feeding just offshore.

From the river viewing platform, the Hutt River Trail (not our route) sets off along the river stopbank towards the Shandon golf course and a view over the estuary, a popular wading and migratory bird watching spot. Royal spoonbills sometimes visit here.

The Esplanade Walkway (our walk) is signposted 'to Korokoro Gateway'. It follows the foreshore on a sealed pathway leaving Hikoikoi reserve and passes between the shingle beach and ❷ **McEwan Park** rugby league ground.

POPULAR PLAYGROUND
Follow the trail to ❸ **Lions Park**, which sits at the western end of Marine Parade, 1 kilometre from the start of the walk. Most in demand here is the multi-coloured children's playground and, at the weekend, the model railway operated by a local club.

From the playground continue westwards and enjoy the sculptures, on the far side of the Lions Park kiosk, placed here by Hutt Valley Community Arts, an organisation that promotes and encourages art in the region. Of special interest is the mosaic seat. You may be lucky enough to time your walk to coincide with a summer story-telling time here.

Pause on the harbour-viewing platforms or take a walk on the boardwalks to the sandy beach, and observe the rich, golden-coloured native pingao, or golden sand sedge, holding the low sand dunes together. Pingao is valued by Maori for weaving but is becoming harder to find, partly because of competition from introduced sand-binding plants such as marram grass, and is now listed as a 'vulnerable species'. The planting of pingao here is just one of the many council planting projects carried out along the foreshore since 1997.

The next sculpture to admire is *Salute*, two oars soaring skyward that 'salute' all travellers, past and future, to arrive or depart this shoreline. The work of sculptor John Calvert, commissioned by the Hutt City Council, stands across from Cuba Street.

Another 100 metres on brings you face-to-face with history – the ❹ **Cross of Iona**, which commemorates the establishment in 1840 of the Presbyterian Church in New Zealand.

Close to the Cross of Iona is the ❺ **Petone Settlers Museum**. The museum building started life in 1939 as the Wellington Centennial Memorial Building and Bathing Pavilion. The bathing pavilion was established as a museum in 1977 and the entire building was refurbished in 1988. The museum is worth a visit.

Beyond the museum is another zany little development, sometimes called ❻ **One Thousand Hand Park**. Take a look at the artwork on the ground here, which encompasses no fewer than 1000 hand prints from local school children – yet another initiative of the Petone Foreshore Steering Group and the Hutt Valley Arts Community.

Local artist Phil Waddington collaborated with local polytechnic welding students to create the fish, eels, seahorse and seashells sculpture that hides the public toilets. If you're hot and bothered, or fancy a swim and want to wash the salt water away, take a break under the public showers installed behind this sculpture. Coin-operated barbecues and picnic tables are also located here.

> **PETONE SETTLERS MUSEUM**
> Open 12 pm–4 pm Tuesday–Friday,
> 1 pm–5 pm weekends and public holidays
> Free admission
> Phone 0-4-568 8373
> This museum of local social and industrial history also has a database of European families who settled the region between 1839 and 1895.

CONSERVING COASTAL PLANTS

Moving on . . . the low-growing plantings along this part of the foreshore include some of the rarest native plants in Wellington. Look for one of the native anisotome plants with their distinctive carrot-top look, and for the bright-magenta, winter-flowering *Hebe speciosa*. This coastal cliff plant no longer grows naturally in Wellington and is categorised as vulnerable throughout the rest of New Zealand. Another rarity, *Euphorbia glauca*, is growing well here on the foreshore after being propagated from just three plants growing on Kapiti Island. Ground-covering *Pimelia prostrata* (New Zealand daphne) is also now extremely rare in Wellington. These species have been propagated by the Hutt City Council's nursery at Percy Scenic Reserve, which has become a specialist haven for some of New Zealand's most endangered plants.

Hutt City Council is part of a Wellington plant conservation network, the first of its kind in the country to involve the community in conservation of threatened plants. Staff from botanical gardens, local and regional councils and the Department of Conservation are collaborating on plant conservation initiatives – almost 200 native plant species are regarded as threatened in the Wellington area.

More 'free form' landscaping and artwork add interest and fun to this little area, next to the **❼ Heretaunga Boating Club**. Past the boating and rowing clubs, the white railings of Petone Wharf extend into the harbour, reaching for deeper waters. This is the second wharf; the first was built in 1883 and used primarily for meat transportation by the Gear Meat Company, a major Petone business for many years. When the original wharf fell into disrepair arguments over the need for a second wharf lasted several years. The replacement was finally built in 1909 but has been little used, as road and rail development provided Petone with other transport links. Nevertheless, the wharf is a popular fishing and swimming spot.

According to Petone Settlers Museum, it was in the vicinity of the wharf that the *Aurora*, the New Zealand Company ship, arrived with its first load of immigrant settlers on 22 January 1840. The settlers came ashore in longboats under the watchful eye of Te Atiawa chief Te Puni, who lived at Pito-one pa, just along the foreshore at Korokoro.

The last part of this walk leads from the wharf to the pa site, now known as **❽ Korokoro Gateway**, by continuing along the Esplanade Trail, well hidden here from the busy roadway by clever landscaping and plantings.

The chief Te Puni is represented at Korokoro Gateway by a colourful, contemporary carving created by a Te Atiawa descendant. Korokoro Gateway, named for the stream that enters the harbour just beyond the carpark, has also been landscaped by the council and the local community. Just to the east of the large carpark there is a series of little seating platforms. These are placed here for good reason: council research shows that one of the most popular activities on the foreshore is eating takeaways from nearby fish and chip shops!

To get back to your car retrace your steps along the waterfront or perhaps take a detour down Jackson Street, Petone's zany main street. Alternatively you can catch the Eastbourne bus back to the other end of the Esplanade.

REFRESHMENTS

A kiosk, selling snacks and ice creams near Lions Park, is open most days in the middle of the day. A mobile coffee cart offers espresso at weekends. Across the Esplanade are restaurants and cafés, with more located in Jackson Street.

KOROKORO VALLEY
The hidden glen

This gentle, delightful track through Korokoro valley to Korokoro dam is extremely popular with walkers, joggers

START/FINISH
Cornish Street road-end, Petone

DISTANCE/TIME
7.5 km, an easy 2 to 3 hours (return)

ACCESS
As you come from Wellington, Cornish Street turns left off SH 2 just past the Petone motorway exit. Be prepared to turn immediately after passing beneath the overbridge.
Petone railway station is 1 km from Cornish Street. Use the footbridge north of the station to cross SH 2 and walk back towards Wellington to Cornish Street.

WHAT TO EXPECT UNDERFOOT A mix of metal and dirt track that in places is a bit narrow, rocky and muddy, plus a few steps.
DOGS Must be on a leash
MOUNTAIN BIKES Yes

and bikers. At least it's popular with those who know about it. Such is its 'hidden' location, many people drive through the heart of Petone's industrial area without having any idea about the forest-filled valley nestled little more than 100 metres from the main road.

It wasn't always so, for the Korokoro Stream was known about by early developers who saw its value as a water supply. The stream flows down a splinter faultline between the hills of Horokiwi and Korokoro, and empties into Wellington Harbour at the western end of Petone Beach.

In 1886 the Wellington Woollen Manufacturing Company opened a mill at the end of what is now Cornish Street, and tapped into the stream's

KOROKORO VALLEY 95

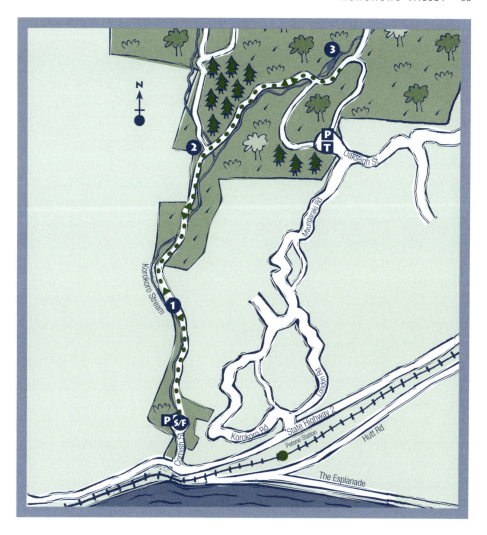

WALK KEY

❶ Old mill dam   **❷** Korokoro Forks   **❸** Korokoro dam and reservoir

water supply, hence the local name of Mill Stream. In 1903 the Petone Borough Council stepped in to procure this water source for town water supply. The stream was dammed in its upper reaches, a pipeline installed through the valley's narrow gorges, and a second dam built further down-valley to create a separate water supply for the mill.

The use of Korokoro water for town supply ended in 1964 (when it was deemed unfit for human consumption!), and the mill closed in 1968. The two dams silted up, pipes rusted and noxious weeds invaded the valley's lower reaches. Somewhat ironically, the forest in the upper valley that was protected for water catchment purposes is now one of the most significant stands of mature native forest remaining in Wellington.

The story gets better. When Belmont Regional Park was formed in 1977, Korokoro valley was incorporated into the park and a foot track built along the old pipeline. In stepped the local residents, determined to restore some natural qualities to the lower valley. Since 1994, these people have worked with park staff to rid the valley of its weeds and replant native species. New plantings of native trees, such as ngaio, have quickly become well established.

Since 2005, the Korokoro Valley track has been the southern end of Puke Ariki Trail, a 22 kilometre walk and bikeway that traverses the Belmont hills to Dry Creek, at the northern end of the Regional Park.

THE WALK

At the end of Cornish Street cross the footbridge, pass the regional park information sign and follow the metalled track alongside Korokoro Stream. Despair not; the blackberry and gorse beside the track here soon gives way to regenerating native forest as you make your way up the valley.

After just a few minutes you'll see a large steel grille across the stream. Continue along the narrow foot track which heads to the right of the grille, then leaves the open clearing and continues through a profusion of native shrubbery, dominated by rangiora and the distinctive, heart-shaped kawakawa. Bigger trees here include karaka; look also for native fuchsia, with its reddish, papery bark trunks standing out among the softer greens and browns of other vegetation.

As the track crosses a small footbridge the valley opens out a little, allowing a good view of valley sides covered with regenerating native shrubs and trees. Listen for the trilling song of little grey warblers (riroriro) and look for piwakawaka, friendly fantails flitting above the stream surface in search of flying insects. Bellbirds are here too, growing in number as the native forest regenerates.

The track climbs a very gentle uphill grade into the valley, the exception being the occasional small bluff to climb up and over. The old pipeline, which once carried water from the

PERCY SCENIC RESERVE

This little oasis is hidden in the bush beside busy SH 2 at Petone. The Percy family operated a mill here from 1851, and their keen interest in gardening and conservation has left a legacy of native forest and landscaped gardens. Native species as well as rhododendrons and camellias surround formal lawns. There is also a duck pond, aviary, water wheel, fernery, picnic areas, and even a little cave stocked with cave weta (bring a torch). A plant nursery at the reserve has a collection of some of New Zealand's rarest species.

The reserve, which was one of the first scenic reserves established in New Zealand, also forms the base of a kohekohe forest gully which is part of a bird corridor from Eastbourne to Belmont Regional Park. Paths encircle the reserve's flat, formal garden area and steep bush tracks explore the kohekohe forest-covered hillside.

For access, the reserve's main car park entrance is from Dowse Drive. Travelling on SH2, turn onto Dowse Drive (signposted to Maungaraki) and the car park is on the left, about 400 metres from the turn off. Alternatively, there are bush tracks leading downhill to the formal gardens from Stanhope Street. If travelling by train, get off at Petone, cross the overbridge and walk north.

Korokoro Reservoir, can be seen from time to time. About 20 minutes from the start the remains of the ❶ old mill dam straddle a narrow cleft in the Korokoro Stream gorge. Just past the dam some particularly impressive karaka, mahoe and mamaku tree ferns cover the steep hillsides across the gorge. Near here the track swings right, then after five minutes crosses over a bridge to the true right, or south side, of the stream.

THE GOOD SIDE OF GORSE
Where the valley widens a little, younger regenerating shrubs are starting to dominate on the previously gorse-covered hills. It may be a weed, but gorse is also a good nitrogen-fixing plant, which helps the natives become established.

As the track enters a grove of old pine trees, a turn-off to Belmont trig, via Baked Beans Bend is signposted to the left. This junction is known as

❷ **Korokoro Forks**, where the east and west branches of the Korokoro meet. Ignore the left-hand option, instead crossing the bridge over the west branch of the stream and continuing straight ahead beside the east branch.

Notice how the native regeneration is thriving beneath the old pines. A little further on, older native forest becomes dominant. The sky is hidden as tall tawa and rewarewa trees tower above the stream, their long trunks covered with ferns, vines, creepers and kiekie. Beneath this profusion of plants the Korokoro Stream gurgles on.

In the midst of the tallest forest the track crosses back to the north side of the stream to a little grassy clearing. Detour to the left, down a few steps, to a seat and a view of the Korokoro Stream cascading down the old spillway of Korokoro dam.

Return to the main track and climb the big steps for 50 metres to arrive at a track junction. Veer left and descend 30 metres to ❸ **Korokoro dam and reservoir** – and a grassy clearing and seats. It's a pleasant picnic spot, one likely to be shared with resident mallard ducks who will undoubtedly show keen interest in any bread scraps you have with you.

A bridge with railings extends for about 30 metres across the dam; youngsters will need to be watched! The bridge is a good spot from which to look around the valley sides, clothed with tall forest. In early spring the rusty red flowers of rewarewa are a fine feature.

It's time to retrace your steps to Cornish Street; or if you have the time and the energy, you can continue on to Belmont trig as described in the following walk. There's also an alternative exit, signposted beside the dam, which climbs to Oakleigh Street should you have transport organised to collect you.

REFRESHMENTS

There is a great selection of cafés and restaurants in Petone, in Jackson Street and along the Esplanade.

BELMONT TRIG
Beautiful bush and inspiring views

START/FINISH
Belmont Regional Park, Oakleigh Street entrance, Maungaraki

DISTANCE/TIME
8.5 km, 3.5–4 hours (loop)

ACCESS
By car, turn left off SH 2 onto Dowse Drive and drive for 2.6 km then, just past the Maungaraki shops, turn left onto Oakleigh Street. The park entrance and carpark are marked 500 m along Oakleigh Street.
By public transport, catch a number 53 bus from Petone railway station.
NOTE This walk (except for the Oakleigh Street to Korokoro dam section) is closed for lambing from August to November.

WHAT TO EXPECT UNDERFOOT Shingle, earth and grass surfaces, some steps, and many tree roots! Steep and slippery in parts with a few stream crossings.
DOGS No (part of this walk passes through park farmland)
MOUNTAIN BIKES Yes

Three special things about Wellington are the mature native forest stands that survive close to the city, the proliferation of native forest regeneration, and the number of great vantage points where stunning views extend beyond Wellington's picturesque harbour to the mountain ranges and coastline of central New Zealand. This walk has the best of all three.

It is a reasonably arduous climb and is exposed to gusts of wind from all directions but the rewards are great. Belmont trig has a 360-degree view that takes in the Tararua Range in the north, the Kaikoura ranges in the south, and all that lies in between.

Pick your day! There is little point in climbing

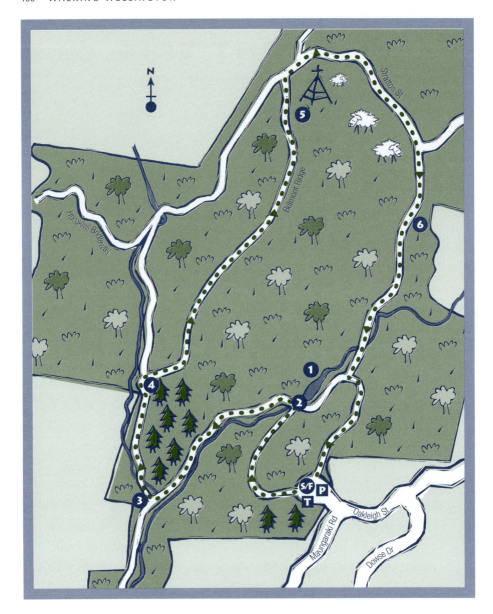

WALK KEY

1. Korokoro dam and reservoir 2. Bridge 3. Korokoro Forks
4. Baked Beans Bend 5. Trig 6. Mature native forest

to the trig if your view is obscured by cloud or if the weather is such that you become exposed to high winds, bitter cold and poor visibility. Be prepared for cold and suddenly changing conditions on the open tops. Take warm, windproof clothing, even if the weather is sunny at the carpark.

The lower part of the walk explores the old Korokoro dam and the upper reaches of Korokoro valley. Because this was a water catchment area for Petone for 60 years, the forest was left intact and remains as one of the largest surviving stands of mature native forest in Wellington.

Other landscapes – younger regenerating native shrubs and trees, pine plantations and farmland – also feature on this walk.

THE WALK

From the carpark, take the track signposted to Korokoro dam and Belmont trig that heads southwards through young pine trees and various grassy clearings.

The shingle track enters the bush and descends quite steeply towards Korokoro dam. Several wooden bridges cross little gullies and are cantilevered against the sides of bluffs, which are generally smothered with a healthy mix of ferns, creepers and shrubs. As you descend the forest grows taller, from a regenerating association of mahoe, rangiora and hangehange shrubs to lofty tawa and rewarewa trees. Kohia (New Zealand passionfruit) vines are tangled throughout, and in gullies nikau palms and kiekie climbing plants flourish in the damp conditions.

At ❶ **Korokoro dam** and reservoir our circuit turns left, but you might like to detour to the right first and descend 30 metres to look at the dam itself, nestled in a basin of predominantly rewarewa forest beside a small, grassy picnic area. (A more detailed description of the dam and its history is in the Korokoro Valley walk, starting on page 94.)

To continue, cross the ❷ **bridge** over Korokoro Stream just downstream of the dam and follow the narrow track along the old water pipeline beside the stream, which is at times cut into the small bluffs that line this narrow gorge. (This section is also part of the Korokoro Valley walk.)

Enjoy this pretty and easy section of the circuit as it winds through a mix of tall native forest, smaller regenerating shrubs and old pine trees. About 15 to 20 minutes from Korokoro dam the track arrives at ❸ **Korokoro Forks**. Cross the bridge over the west branch of the Korokoro Stream, then turn right onto the track marked 'Belmont Trig via Baked Beans Bend'.

ROCK HOPPING

For 15 minutes or so the track follows the west branch of the stream, through a mix of native and old pine forest, with several stream crossings involved. With careful use of judiciously placed rocks and at one point a 'fallen tree' bridge you might be able to keep your feet dry! Chances are you will easily hear approaching mountain bikers – riding through streams such as this tends to bring on their loudest whoops and yeehas.

After the sixth stream negotiation the play is over – and the climbing begins in earnest. The first 50-metre climb heads to the right from the stream bed beside an old fenceline, and leads to a grassy flat known curiously as ❹ **Baked Beans Bend**. Surrounded by hinau and tawa forest, this is one of the designated camping areas of Belmont Regional Park, although no facilities are provided.

From the flat a further short climb leads to a track junction and stile and gate, where the Horokiwi Bridleway heads left. This provides access for horse riders to the Belmont tops. Our route crosses the stile and continues climbing what is known as Belmont Ridge or Main Ridge. Expect to meet mountain bikers, particularly on weekends and holidays.

The grassy, dirt and at times rocky track climbs out of the valley, sidling around the ridge through alternate open areas and fast-growing native regeneration. With the help of plantings by volunteer conservation groups, both here at Belmont and throughout the region, and with no further disturbance by such events as fire, the notorious gorse-covered hills of Wellington should soon become a phenomenon of the past.

Mahoe and rewarewa are particularly prolific trees on this walk. These natives grow early in the cycle of regeneration. The tawa and scattered podocarp trees in the upper reaches of the Korokoro valley make up what is known as climax forest, the final stage of the lengthy regeneration process.

SHADY RESPITE

About halfway to the trig, after more climbing through fairly open country, a patch of cool, shady bush brings welcome relief. It also hides a panoramic view that is revealed as the track emerges into the open. As they are wont to do, the views on this climb expand as height is gained.

In the final 200 metres or so before the trig the track climbs through more stunted, higher-altitude wind-shorn native forest. Note the brighter green of the stunted miro trees, then the dominant tawa and mahoe, their host trunks and branches entwined with epiphytic vines and creepers.

Further on, take a closer look at the reddish leaves of the horopito (pepperwood) shrubs lining the track. Crush a leaf and taste it, and you will discover the reason for the name pepperwood. This unpalatable species often survives in forests that are otherwise eaten away by possums and deer. The divaricated coprosma, also lining the track here, is also unpalatable to animals.

The track emerges into the open and crosses a stile to reach the ❺ **trig** (457 metres).

Take a well-earned rest and turn a full circle for the view. It encompasses the Tararua Range (New Zealand's first forest park), wildlife sanctuary Kapiti Island, Plimmerton and a glimpse of the twin harbours of Porirua and Pauatahanui, Cook Strait, Marlborough Sounds and Tapuae o Uenuku, the highest peak of the Kaikoura ranges, which stands tall beyond the suburb of Karori. Wellington's harbour nestles in the foreground. From this vantage point, no one could refute the claim this is one of the most scenic harbours in the world!

It's easy to visualise the paths of the two taniwha, Ngake (who broke through the landlocked harbour to create the harbour entrance) and Whataitai, caught by the tide and lying stranded, thus joining Miramar Peninsula to Wellington. Closer still Hutt Valley – river, city and suburbs – is set out beneath the Belmont Hills.

There are no signs at the trig, but the grassy track is obvious, zigzagging down the other side of the trig from where you came up. After about 250 metres, just past the bridleway track which turns to the left, there is a stile then a second track junction.

THE LONG DESCENT

A left-hand turn here leads to Cannons Head, another high viewpoint one hour's walk away, but our route continues straight ahead on the track marked 'Stratton Street'. This descends through farmland, away from the bush of Korokoro valley and away from city views. The outlook now, of tree-lined farm paddocks, is distinctly rural.

After about 25 minutes the Stratton Street track goes straight ahead, but you need to turn right at the sign to Oakleigh Street. The grassy track sidles around the hillside (look for orange marker posts) then climbs a stile, enters the bush and descends, steeply at times, into the Korokoro headwaters.

Here the walk passes some of the most impressive ❻ **mature native forest** in the valley: tall tawa dominate but a few kahikatea and rimu also tower above the forest canopy. The track follows the Korokoro Stream, with little bridges, steps and, at times, a thick leafy carpet of distinctive long, narrow, serrated rewarewa and smaller tawa leaves underfoot, then comes to a junction.

A right turn heads back to Korokoro dam, but to go directly to the Oakleigh Street carpark, veer left and climb gradually through the forest past some impressively big trees, until the track emerges from the bush on the opposite side of the carpark from where you first began.

REFRESHMENTS

There is a great selection of cafés and restaurants in Petone, in Jackson Street and along the Esplanade.

DAYS BAY
Beech trees, rata and orchids

A magnificent stand of mature beech and rata forest, probably the only forest of such quality in New Zealand growing so close to a major city, is the special feature of this walk. There are other delights: stunning forest-framed views of the harbour and city, native flowers (depending on the season), the story of the 'possum busters' and the delightful harbourside ambience of Days Bay and Williams Park. And it's all just an easy ferry trip or 20-minute drive from central Wellington.

If you are keen to go bush tramping, but the big mountain ranges are too far away or perhaps too daunting, then pop on over to Days Bay and explore this walk. But follow the directions carefully. The complicated network of tracks in these hills is confusing and people have been known to lose their way!

Like many native forests, those along the eastern harbour

START/FINISH
Williams Park, Days Bay

DISTANCE/TIME
5.5 km, 2–3 hours (loop)

ACCESS
Williams Park is across the road from the Days Bay wharf on Wellington Harbour. Walk into the park and go to the right-hand (south) end of the duck pond. The track is signposted at the bush edge. Vehicle gates are closed at dusk.
The Eastbourne bus and East by West Ferry (Queens Wharf to Days Bay) take you directly to Williams Park.

WHAT TO EXPECT UNDERFOOT Forest tramping track, steep in parts, some steps
DOGS Must be on a leash
MOUNTAIN BIKES No

106 WALKING WELLINGTON

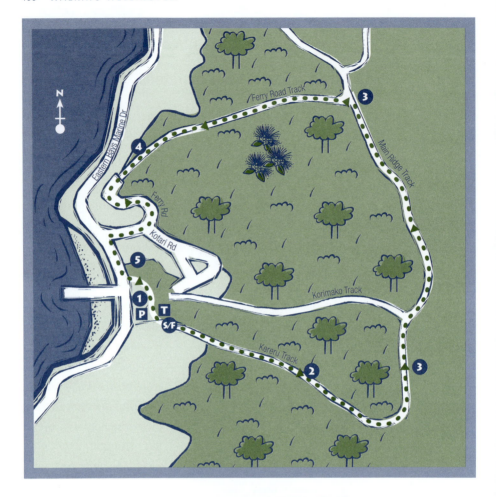

WALK KEY

❶ Williams Park   **❷** Seat and lookout   **❸** Main ridge
❹ Former pine plantation   **❺** Wellesley College

have suffered ravages by possums. But a two-year volunteer effort by the 'possum busters' – members of the local community working with Hutt City Council – saw a substantial reduction in possums and an increase in bird life and plant flowering.

The East Harbour Environment Association has since embarked on a programme called MIRO (Mainland Island Rehabilitation Operation) to rid the area of pests. This has

WILLIAMS PARK

Since the late 1800s Williams Park at Days Bay has been a place for weekend picnics and family fun. The park features a large grassy area, duck pond, pétanque, tennis courts, picnic areas that can be booked by groups and the Pavilion café. The current pavilion is the third built on the site; the first – a grand old building – was completed in 1898. Across the road there is opportunity for safe swimming in the harbour, plus a yacht and sea kayak hire service in summer.

involved hours of walking up and down forested spurs and gullies, in all weathers, checking and setting traps and monitoring results. As you walk through a forest ablaze with crimson-flowering rata in summer, when the tui song resounds, when native mistletoe and orchids flourish, you can thank these dedicated local conservationists.

This walk is in East Harbour Regional Park, which is managed by Greater Wellington, the regional council.

THE WALK

This circuit climbs the Kereru Track to the Main Ridge Track (which follows the main, forested ridge behind the eastern bay settlements), then returns to the harbour's edge via Ferry Road Track.

The walk starts at the bush edge at the south end of the ❶ **Williams Park** duck pond. At first the track is very wide, as it follows the north side of a small stream through forest filled with mamaku tree ferns, kiekie and rata vines. After about 10 minutes a track to Korimako Road heads left, but you need to continue straight ahead, following the signs indicating 'to Ridge Track'. After passing the remains of an old weir that was once part of a Days Bay water-supply system, the track steepens and enters beech forest. There are at least two of the five New Zealand beech species here, black beech and hard beech, surrounded by a profusion of other native plants.

By your feet, notice the bright-green, ground-covering kidney ferns, named for their distinctive shape. Also worth looking for are native orchids hanging in magnificent clumps from tree trunks and branches. Twenty species of native orchid grow in the eastern harbour forests, though many are less visible than the showy, summer-flowering *Earina mucronata* and autumn-flowering *Earina autumnalis*, which is also the most scented of all the native orchids.

The track continues its relentless, upward haul, climbing onto a spur with another stream now flowing on your left. While the stream gullies are filled with a profusion of big trees – rewarewa, beech and mamaku ferns – the forest floor on the spur is comparatively open.

About halfway up a welcome ❷ **seat** provides an outlook over one particularly open area, a legacy of the Wahine storm of 1968, when the forest was badly damaged by ferocious winds. Young beech trees are now showing good signs of growth, but in the meantime the open forest allows a great view looking back across the harbour to Wellington city. Continue upwards, past other track junctions, still following the signs 'to Ridge Track'.

RATA RESPLENDENT

As you climb, rata begins to make its presence felt. Northern rata often embarks on its long life journey as an epiphyte growing on host trees. As its roots reach the ground and the host tree dies, the rata trunk takes form. Some of the best rata specimens in Wellington grow here in the heads of the Days Bay streams. They are seen at their best when flowering, between December and January. Other rata vine species, such as the winter-flowering fulgens rata, also grow here, covering the trunks of the host trees.

The way ahead is obvious: just stay on the highest point between the two gullies and continue walking up. The steep grade eases closer to the top of the spur, where vegetation on the forest floor thickens with mingimingi and putaputaweta shrubs and distinctive lancewoods.

When the track reaches the ❸ **main ridge**, turn left and follow the well-defined track north along the main ridge. The big things to notice here are the huge trees – rata and beech mainly, with the occasional lofty rimu. The shining reflection of aluminium wrapped around the trunks of some of these larger trees will no doubt attract your attention. This is an anti-possum measure, in place to prevent northern rata leaves appearing on possum dinner plates.

On calm days even the silence is big, broken only by the busy chatter and song of native forest birds: grey warblers, fantails and tiny riflemen. New Zealand falcon are also present in this forest. Looking outwards, take time to enjoy the contrasting glimpses of the capital city on one side and, to the east, the forest-clad hills of the Rimutaka Range.

After about 30 minutes on the main ridge, Korimako Track turns down to the left. It's a good track, but after the effort of the climb it seems a shame to drop down again to Days Bay so soon, so stay with us and continue a little further along the main ridge.

YOUNGER FOREST

The forest changes at this point, from the mature rata and beech giants to a younger forest of predominantly kamahi trees. This is one of the areas of the Days Bay forest that have been burnt by wildfires over the past 100 years, and kamahi has since become established in place of the original beech forest. The kamahi's thin, white trunks line the track, which undulates, fairly steeply at times, along the main ridge. Note the big tree ferns flourishing in damp low sections of the ridge.

About 30 minutes beyond the Korimako Track junction, as you arrive at a small open area, turn left onto the track signposted to Ferry Road. (Main Ridge Track continues along above Lowry Bay to eventually meet with the Wainuiomata Hill Road.) Our track descends quite steeply, first through beech forest and then a thick profusion of regenerating native trees, shrubs and ferns.

If you are walking in midsummer, look for the blaze of crimson from flowering rata trees in the gully to the south of the track. Eastern bays residents, who have been leading the war against possums in this forest, report that such flowering has improved dramatically since the bush-browsing possums have been knocked back.

As you near Days Bay the track bursts into the open, as it leaves the native forest and passes through a ❹ **former pine plantation**, planted during the Depression and cleared in 2005. Enjoy the dramatic views, looking south over Eastbourne towards the harbour entrance, across the harbour to Matiu (Somes) Island and Wellington city, and back along the ridgeline you have just walked. The felled tree

REFRESHMENTS

A picnic or café stop at Days Bay is a most agreeable way to end your walk. Brush the mud from your shoes and replenish! The Pavilion at Williams Park offers everything from ice creams and takeaways to sit-down café meals, and other Days Bay cafés are located just along the waterfront.

stumps make good seats, although the native regeneration here promises to hide this outlook in years to come.

About 30 to 40 minutes after leaving the main ridge, the track emerges from the trees onto Ferry Road. Follow the road for 750 metres as it winds down to the harbour edge. You will pass walkway signs along the way, but our circuit takes you directly to the harbour, where you can choose to walk the remaining 300 metres or so back to Williams Park along the footpath or the beach.

A LITTLE BIT OF HISTORY

Of interest along the waterfront is the lovely old building of ❺ **Wellesley College**. This was originally Days Bay House, a hotel built in 1903. It became Croydon School in 1914, and the private boys' college became established in 1940. Just before the school entrance, note the garden of sand-binding plants – the native pingao a golden contrast to the introduced marram grass.

BUTTERFLY CREEK
Of beech forest and Butterfly Creek

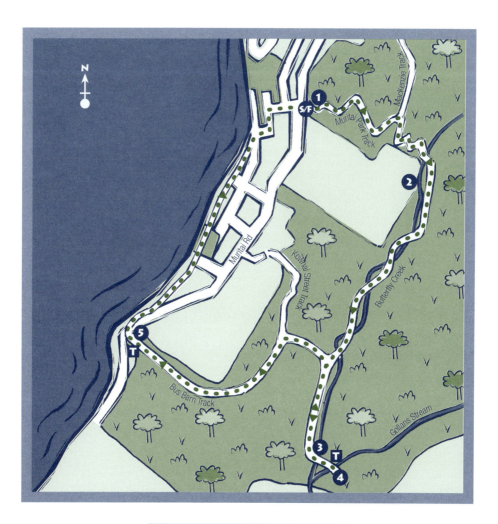

WALK KEY

❶ Muritai Park ❷ Butterfly Creek ❸ Kahikatea tree
❹ Butterfly Creek clearing ❺ Bus Barn

START/FINISH
Muritai Park, Muritai Road, Eastbourne

DISTANCE/TIME
5.5 km, 2.5–3 hours (loop)

ACCESS
The Muritai Park entrance is between 259 and 261 Muritai Road, Eastbourne. The walk returns to the coastline at the Eastbourne 'Bus Barn', 1.8 km further along Muritai Road.
Eastbourne buses pass both of these points. Alternatively take the East by West ferry from Wellington's Queens Wharf to the Days Bay wharf and catch the Eastbourne bus from there. Days Bay is 2 km from the Muritai Park entrance.

WHAT TO EXPECT UNDERFOOT Good quality walking track. Some road walking required if returning to a vehicle.
DOGS Must be on a leash
MOUNTAIN BIKES No

For many years Wellington families have been walking to the small forest clearing near Butterfly Creek in the Eastbourne hills for picnics, swimming and overnight camping expeditions. The walk involves climbing to the ridgeline behind Eastbourne (great harbour views!) then dropping into the forest-filled valley behind and following Butterfly Creek to reach the clearing, by its confluence with Gollans Stream. The mature beech forest in this valley is a special feature. This is the sort of forest one would normally expect in the remote back country, not in such close proximity to one of New Zealand's major cities.

The area here is in the East Harbour Regional Park, which is managed by Greater Wellington, the regional council. However the track network and general well-being of the forest is largely a result of over 70 years' volunteer effort by a committed group of local residents, the 'Eastbourne Forest Rangers'.

Since the 1930s the Rangers have been involved in fighting bush fires, constructing and maintaining tracks, search and rescue, weed control and revegetation work, showing an outstanding and unwavering commitment to the welfare of the hills backing their homes.

In 1999 they and others in the local

community became involved in the Eastern Bays MIRO programme (see page 106). An area of 130 hectares of the Eastbourne hills, including the area of this walk, is being intensively trapped to rid the forest of possums and predators such as stoats and rats. Native birds that benefit from this include tui, kereru, fantails and riflemen, while the presence of rare karearea (New Zealand falcon) in these hills is particularly notable.

While Butterfly Creek is a popular destination and the tracks are obvious and well formed, people have been known to get lost in this area. Keep to the track. You may notice small pink triangles on trees along the walk. These are not direction markers – they indicate trapping lines through the forest for pest control workers and local volunteers.

Four tracks – the MacKenzie, Muritai Park, Kowhai Street and Bus Barn Tracks – climb from Eastbourne and link up to reach Butterfly Creek. I have chosen the Muritai Park and Bus Barn Tracks for this circuit; they offer, in general, a more gradual grade and comprise a fine selection of views and forest types.

THE WALK

From 259 Muritai Road follow the walkway sign and walk 50 metres through to ❶ **Muritai Park**, a little grassy clearing surrounded by native forest where several titoki, fuchsia and karaka trees have been banded to prevent possum browsing.

The track enters the forest and climbs in a series of long zigzags to the top of the ridge. Ignore a side-track signposted 'Lookout' and continue upwards: good views of Eastbourne and the harbour will open up as you climb. About 10 minutes from the start the first beech trees appear, a mix of hard and black beech species growing amongst manuka trees.

About 100 metres before the ridgeline the track breaks out of tall forest to reveal great views over the lower-growing native shrubs to Wellington Harbour, the Belmont hills and Mt Kaukau. In the foreground the nature reserve of Matiu (Somes) Island nestles in its isolated harbour spot. There's a seat handily placed from which you can rest and enjoy this view.

REMOTE RIDGELINES

At the top of the ridge Muritai Park Track joins with MacKenzie Track, then descends into the valley on the eastern side of the ridge. Suddenly the forest seems far removed from a city so close but now out of sight. As the track descends, gradually at first and then on a steeper grade, outlooks to the east reveal ridgeline after ridgeline of forest-covered ranges.

The track gradually descends for about 15 minutes to the valley floor, then leads alongside ❷ **Butterfly Creek**. As you walk, note the variety of forest plants. The biggest trees are black beech, hinau and rimu growing on the higher terraces and giant kahikatea thriving in the damp soils of the valley floor. Tree ferns are prolific and, in the dark, damp gullies especially, trees are festooned with epiphytic plants and lianes – supplejack vines, large-leafed puka (broadleaf), huge clumps of astelia and the climbing plant kiekie.

Banks lining the track are smothered with the multi-shaded greens of a multitude of ferns, many named for their distinctive shapes. Look for the bright-green kidney ferns, long and narrow fronds of hound's tongue, larger crown ferns and the delicate hen and chicken, named for the small bulbets ('chickens') which sit on the mature fronds ('hens'). If walking in summer, look for the delicately flowered native orchid, *Dendrobium cunninghamii*.

After an easy hour wandering alongside the stream, the track climbs a little and meets with the track from Kowhai Street. Turn left and keep heading down-valley on the good quality, benched track. Beech trees are still dominant; beech litter covers the track and dappled light filters through in the way characteristic of beech forests throughout New Zealand. The rich, deep greens of rimu can be seen scattered along the valley and the track passes close beside a huge ❸ **kahikatea tree**, its host trunk smothered with vines and creepers.

BUTTERFLY CREEK

About 15 minutes from the Kowhai Street junction the track comes to an area of younger beech trees, veers left then crosses a bridge over Gollans Stream to reach the ❹ **Butterfly Creek** clearing.

This little clearing with its tiny swimming hole has been popular since the early 1900s. For more than 10 years from the late 1930s, walkers could buy tea, soft drinks and scones from a kiosk built of tree fern trunks (and later with an iron roof) at the clearing. Today there is nothing left of the kiosk, but there is a toilet and a fine little swimming hole.

To complete the walk, retrace your steps from the Butterfly Creek clearing and take the track signposted to Kowhai Street. This climbs steadily back to the top of the ridge. At the top of the ridge turn left onto the Bus Barn Track. This track is a longer but more gently graded option than Kowhai Street Track. It also passes through some healthy forest regeneration and offers a great view of the harbour entrance and (on a good day) the Kaikoura mountains.

At first the track stays on the ridgeline, threading its way for a time through hedge-like hangehange shrubs. The vegetation along the Bus Barn Track is a typical mix of a young, regenerating forest filled with trees and shrubs such as hangehange, mahoe, kawakawa, kamahi and rangiora, which are among the first to colonise slopes that have been cleared or burned. Exposure to high winds has made these Eastbourne hills particularly susceptible to bush fires, hence the renowned firefighting efforts of a band of Eastbourne volunteers.

After about 700 metres the track leaves the ridge and descends fairly steeply to the ❺ **Bus Barn**. Take care in wet and slippery conditions!

Once back on Muritai Road, either meet with your bus or walk the 1.8 kilometres back to the Muritai Park entrance. As Muritai Road curves away from the harbour, continue beside the coastline if you wish and turn inland onto Karamu Road to arrive back at your starting point.

REFRESHMENTS
Let one of Eastbourne's many cafés tempt you.

PENCARROW HEAD
Lighthouses, lakes and a long coastal walk

START/FINISH
Burdans Gate, 3 km south of Eastbourne

DISTANCE/TIME
18 km, 4–5 hours (return)

ACCESS
By car, drive through the village of Eastbourne and continue 3 km around the coast on Muritai Road to Burdans Gate, at the road-end. There is plenty of parking. Alternatively, take the Eastbourne bus. The Eastbourne Bus Barn depot is on Muritai Road, 400 m from the start of the track. Or take the East by West ferry from Queens Wharf to the Days Bay wharf, then catch the Eastbourne bus from there.

WHAT TO EXPECT UNDERFOOT Mostly shingle road. At Pencarrow Head a foot track and grassy farm track (sometimes muddy) climb to the lighthouse.
DOGS Must be on leash
MOUNTAIN BIKES There will be lots, although there is plenty of room for both walkers and riders

This long but easy walk on the east coast of Wellington Harbour offers stunning seascapes, especially from the historic lighthouse on the headland, a touch of rural landscape and a wetland wildlife reserve. (If you're a biker, this will be an easier option.)

But be warned: the Pencarrow coast is exposed to both the northerly gales that scream down the harbour from Hutt Valley and to the southerly squalls that blast across Cook Strait. Go prepared – take warm, waterproof, windproof clothing.

The long history of ships that have foundered here is testimony to the challenging, changeable conditions of the Pencarrow coast: at least

PENCARROW HEAD 117

WALK KEY

1 Burdans Gate **2** Grassy flat **3** Old wharf **4** Lighthouse
5 Sewer outfall pipe **6** Lake Kohangapiripiri lookout
7 Old lighthouse

40 have been wrecked in the last 150 years. There is little trace of these today, but sobering memories remain intact, particularly of the *Wahine* inter-island ferry, which foundered on Barrett Reef in a ferocious storm in 1968. Winds and sea currents swept the ferry's life rafts and the bodies of all but two of the 51 people who drowned onto this coastline. There is a *Wahine* memorial stone near the road-end carpark.

For many people doing this walk the focal point is the historic lighthouse on the Pencarrow headland. Built in 1859, it was the first lighthouse in New Zealand. However, it was so frequently obscured by fog a second light was built down on the shoreline in 1906.

While seascapes will dominate your outlook as you walk, also worth noting is the coastal forest that survives in these harsh, salty conditions, including some species that normally grow high in the mountains.

Just beyond Pencarrow Head several rare and threatened native plants grow in the wetland environments of two small freshwater lakes. Tucked away behind the headland and sheltered from the stormy coast, these lakes harbour fish, waterfowl and seabirds, and are wildlife reserves. This walk visits Kohangapiripiri, the first of the lakes; the second, Kohangatera, is a further 30 minutes' walk along the coast road.

The Pencarrow coastal route was established only after the 1855 Wellington earthquake raised the shoreline level by about 2 metres. It was initially a stock route to Wairarapa farms and a supply road for the lighthouse. The road is now closed to public vehicles. Council vehicles servicing the Pencarrow sewer outfall or quarry trucks from a quarry beyond Pencarrow Head sometimes disrupt the quiet, though walkers will need to keep more of a wary eye out for speeding bikes, particularly on the weekends. Sheep and cattle are also likely to be encountered, as the surrounding land is farmed.

There are picnic spots along the way and toilets at the start of the walk. Take your own drinking water. Swimming off the beach is not recommended because of strong sea currents and the close proximity of the sewer outfall.

This walk is in East Harbour Regional Park and crosses land owned by Hutt City Council. The Department of Conservation manages the two lake wildlife reserves, while Pencarrow Lighthouse Historic Reserve is administered by the New Zealand Historic Places Trust.

THE WALK

From the carpark, go through ❶ **Burdans Gate**, where a private road heads uphill and our route to Pencarrow continues along the coast.

For the first part of the walk native coastal shrubs, interspersed with a fair amount of gorse, cover the roadside banks. Scattered cabbage trees stand above a dense and matted mix of shrubs and creepers – twiggy *Coprosma propinqua*, tangled pohuehue and native spinach.

On the seaward side introduced yellow-flowered horned poppies grow over the open shingle. In the water the enriching mix of salt and fresh Hutt River water has created a habitat for a great diversity of plants and algae. Sea lettuce, Neptune's necklace and red algae live in the storm-drenched rock pools. Beds of kelp lie offshore.

Watch the water as you walk; chances are you will see various species of shags out fishing or perhaps just resting on a sunny rock, and flocks of gulls working the water together. You may even be so lucky with the timing of your walk as to spot a visiting marine mammal cruising by – pods of dolphins and orcas (killer whales) are regular visitors to Wellington Harbour.

No particular landmark features stand out on this coastal road. Camp Bay, the wide, sweeping bay at the start of the walk, is so named because local residents once came here for summer camping holidays. The next bay is known as Paraonui. In earlier times there was a Maori fishing camp here, and today there is a ❷ **grassy flat** with a picnic table across the road from the beach. It's a pleasant spot, sheltered by surrounding shrubs and with a charming outlook. At the water's edge 100 metres further on look carefully for three rotting piles. These are all that remain of an ❸ **old wharf** that was built when rockfill from here was barged across the harbour for Wellington city's waterfront reclamations.

HISTORIC POINTS

The road continues round two promontories, Hinds Point (named after Reverend Hinds, a supporter of the New Zealand Company) and Inconstant Point, where the sailing ship *Inconstant* came aground in 1849. The *Inconstant* wreck became known as Plimmer's Ark (see page 20).

Inconstant Point is the best spot on the walk to see the rocks of Barrett Reef, jutting ominously above the water in the middle of the harbour entrance. These are the rocks that were the demise of the *Wahine*, although the ferry sank further inside the harbour, just off the coast of Seatoun.

This is also the best spot to watch ships or, more likely, one of today's inter-island ferries coming in or out of the harbour. These big vessels steer well clear of Barrett Reef and consequently can seem close enough to touch as they pass Inconstant Point.

Among the wind-shorn vegetation clinging to the cliffs along here are clumps of speargrass and mountain flax, plants that normally grow in cold, harsh mountain environments.

Don't be deterred from enjoying the coastal scenery by the sign here warning of potential pollution from the sewer outfall; you're still some distance from it.

About 200 metres past Inconstant Point a narrow, signposted track climbs away from the road towards a stile and the old lighthouse. Ignore this for now, continuing instead along the coast road around the base of Pencarrow Head and past the newer, working ❹ **lighthouse** at shore level.

As the road curves around the headland the outlook changes significantly. Here the full fury of the Southern Ocean can make its presence felt, adding to the drama of occasional rocks falling from the cliff tops. It is not a place to linger, so continue around the next point, where a sweeping vista opens up, looking across the south coast to Fitzroy Bay,

farmland and distant Baring Head.

Concentrate on the view here, for chances are other senses will suddenly be assailed here by odours emanating from the Hutt City ❺ **sewer outfall pipe**, which by now you will probably have noticed thrusting several hundred metres out to sea. It's a blot on the landscape, the seascape and certainly at times the smellscape. Fortunately there are better things ahead.

Just beyond the pipe, a farm track climbs away from the road to the left, where a signpost indicates Lake Kohangapiripiri and Old Pencarrow Light. The road continues around the coast to Lake Kohangatera, the shipwreck remains of the small steamer *Paiaka*, Fitzroy Bay and Baring Head.

Our circuit heads up the farm road to Lake Kohangapiripiri, but first detour some 50 metres along the road to where a sign placed on the fenceline explains the significant natural history of this area, in particular of the two dune lakes.

SHELTERED WETLAND

Follow the farm track, through the gate or over the stile to Lake Kohangapiripiri; a sudden contrast from the wildness of the south coast. Like Lake Kohangatera, Kohangapiripiri has formed behind a raised gravel-and-sand bank uplifted by earthquakes.

LAKES AND WETLANDS

Should you wish to make a full day of this outing, it is possible to walk right around both Lake Kohangapiripiri and Lake Kohangatera, taking in the extensive wetlands at the head of each lake, watching the waterfowl and enjoying splendid outlooks from the open ridgeline the tracks climb between the two lakes. Boardwalks cross the wetlands, through a variety mix of wetland vegetation – jointed wire rush, raupo, flax and toetoe – while regenerating manuka and kanuka forest edges the shorelines. Greater Wellington Regional Council brochures and information panels at the lakes themselves show this track network, which is suitable for both walking and mountain biking.

Starting from where Lighthouse Track meets Lake Kohangapiripiri, allow 3.5 to 4.5 hours for a circuit of both lakes, and 1.5 to 2 hours to walk around Lake Kohangapiripiri, via Kohangapiripri and Cameron Ridge Tracks.

Such wetland environments are now rare, and many of the herbs, sedges and rushes that grow around the lake margins are threatened species. Both lakes are registered by the Department of Conservation as nationally important wetlands. Eels, freshwater fish and birds, including breeding colonies of black shag, pukeko, Australasian bittern, spotless crake and pied stilt live in and around the lake. Flocks of seagulls sometimes rest on its calm waters, seeking respite from the Southern Ocean swells. This is also one of the few mainland sites around Wellington where banded dotterel breed.

The track meanders around the southern side of the lake; it can be quite boggy at times. At the south-west corner of the lake, our circuit leads straight ahead towards the Pencarrow Lighthouse track, but first there is a worthy detour to enjoy, should you wish.

Kohangapiriri Track to Cameron Creek Wetland and ❻ **Lake Kohangatera lookout** is signposted on the right. Turn onto this track, cross a small boardwalk, and climb about 250 metres beside the lake to a junction. Veer left and another 100 metres brings you to a delightful outlook across the lake, over the earthquake-raised bank and out to sea.

Return the way you came to continue our circuit, or explore further around Lake Kohangapiripiri and its wetlands if you wish. (For more extensive walks here see Lakes and Wetlands, page 121.)

Back on our original trail at the end of the lake, turn right onto Lighthouse Track and follow the wide, grassy track that climbs gradually into the head of a small valley. After about 600 metres this leads to a stile, and meets the lighthouse track you saw earlier.

Follow the track to the lighthouse as it zigzags and climbs gradually, and great views unfold around you. Take your time, perhaps pausing by the grave of a lighthouse keeper's daughter. It is indeed a lonely, wild and windswept resting place. At the ❼ **old lighthouse**, the views encompass the full extent of Wellington Harbour, looking right into the Hutt River valley. The south coast and Seatoun Peninsula are close at hand, while to the south the Kaikoura ranges, in winter snow-covered, are more than 100 kilometres away. To the east the view extends beyond Lake Kohangapiripiri, nestled among the farmland hills, to Fitzroy Bay and the forest-clad hills of Rimutaka Forest Park.

It's a grand, solitary spot, a place where it's worth thinking about the lighthouse keepers and their families who once lived here. When the first keeper drowned, his wife Mary and her three children stayed on at the job for 10 years.

Continue your contemplation, and enjoyment of the great outlooks, by following the track that heads in a south-east direction from just below the lighthouse, for about 20 minutes, to Bluff Point Lookout.

This walk is completed by returning to the stile below the lighthouse, then descending the short, steepish track to the coastal road and retracing your steps to Burdans Gate. With luck the wind will not have turned to the north!

REFRESHMENTS

Ice creams and snacks are available from a kiosk near the Muritai road-end carpark. It is open 'fine weekends' during summer. Bikes can also be hired here.

For something more substantial, you are spoilt for choice by numerous cafés in Eastbourne and Days Bay.

KAITOKE
Big trees, big river

Pack grandma and the kids, drive just 40 minutes north of downtown Wellington, and take an easy but stunning riverside walk through some magnificent, centuries-old, podocarp forest. Afterwards enjoy a paddle in the Pakuratahi River or a swim in a deep, green, forest-framed pool of the Hutt River, then partake in a picnic or barbecue with the excellent facilities provided at Kaitoke Regional Park.

Because of various water catchment schemes throughout the region, where hills and valleys have been protected from forest clearance to maintain water quality, Wellington is blessed with some fine remnants of native forest. With its magnificent podocarp trees, Kaitoke is one of the most outstanding examples. Huge rimu, matai, miro and kahikatea trees, plus ancient rata trees, most festooned

START/FINISH
Pakuratahi Forks, Kaitoke Regional Park

DISTANCE/TIME
2.5 km, an easy hour (loop)

ACCESS
Kaitoke Regional Park is on SH 2, 46 km north of Wellington city and 7 km from Te Marua. From Wellington, turn left onto Waterworks Road just before the Rimutaka Hill, where the park is clearly signposted. From the park entrance (1 km from the turn-off) drive through the park for 400 m then turn right and drive 1.2 km, then turn left to the Pakuratahi Forks carpark.

WHAT TO EXPECT UNDERFOOT Benched forest track, sealed road, swingbridge. At least 1 km is negotiable by wheelchairs.
DOGS Must be on a leash
MOUNTAIN BIKES No

124 WALKING WELLINGTON

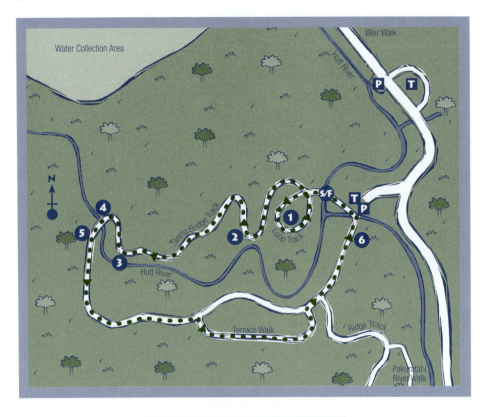

WALK KEY

❶ Loop Walk   **❷** View point   **❸** View point
❹ Flume bridge   **❺** Strainer house   **❻** Clearing

with massive gardens of epiphytic plants and tangled with clambering rata vines and kiekie, tower above a profusion of trees, shrubs, vines and ferns. The forest is easily accessible and the quality of walking track at Kaitoke is particularly good; with a mix of benched track and sealed service road the walk described here is suitable for people of all ages.

Kaitoke Regional Park is located at the bush-clad southern end of the Tararua Range. This is the point where the Hutt River cuts its way out of the steep ranges and flows into the wide valley it has shaped over centuries of flooded meanderings as it has made its way into the Wellington Harbour. The Maori name for the Hutt River is Heretaunga.

In 1939 land at Kaitoke was purchased to collect water for Wellington city. During the 1950s an intake weir was built across a steep gorge of the Hutt River and a flume constructed to carry this water down the river to a strainer house where sticks, stones and leaves were removed from the water. Regional park development began in 1957.

WEIR WALK

This walk, to the Hutt River intake weir, is a short but interesting route close to Pakuratahi Forks. From the carpark, drive or walk uphill 50 metres then turn left and continue 200 metres to the road-end and vehicle barrier. From here it is a 150-metre walk along a service road suitable for wheelchairs to the weir, which collects water for supply to the region. At the weir look across the river to see layers of sedimentary rock that have been laid down horizontally, then uplifted a full 90 degrees by tectonic movement.

THE WALK

The Swingbridge Track is signposted at the far end of the Pakuratahi Forks carpark, beside the park information booth. Walk a few metres along the track to find the swingbridge across the Hutt River.

Cross the bridge above a deep, cool-looking swimming hole and, before heading uphill to the right, turn left for a 250-metre wander around the ❶ **Loop Walk**, where information signs give details about the plants that grow here and explain features of the forest composition. The track name may not be particularly inspirational, but the big trees here certainly are.

Giant rimu, many dripping with epiphytic gardens, are perhaps the most impressive in size and stature.

There are also matai, kahikatea, miro, black beech and rata and, most encouragingly, several young seedling trees of these mighty giants beginning their centuries-long path to maturity.

Having completed this small loop and arrived back near the swingbridge, head up the Swingbridge Track, which zigzags upwards for a few metres then leads on a level grade through the forest. As you walk look up for glimpses of rimu and kahikatea trees towering above the forest canopy.

Look also for the huge clumps of astelia, or perching lily, thriving in their aerial gardens high on the branches of rimu trees. On the ground, note the profusion of hen and chicken ferns that line each side of the track. These ferns are a particular delicacy for browsing animals and their healthy presence here is an indicator of the lack of animal pests such as possums, thanks to the regional council's concerted pest-control efforts. The ferns can be identified by the small 'chickens' that grow on the large fronds ('hens'). Crown fern, identified by its crown-like shape and separate fertile frond, is also prolific.

FROM FERNS TO FOREST GIANTS
Pause at a ❷ **view point** overlooking the Hutt River then continue, climbing very gradually beneath yet more towering rata, rimu and beech trees. When the track comes to a second seat, take the opportunity to rest and admire the rimu tree that dominates your view. Listen for forest dwellers – tui, riflemen, fantails and grey warblers are likely to be in the vicinity.

Look for the occasional dead host tree that's smothered with very much alive rata vines and other epiphytic plants. At a second ❸ **view point** (where a protective barrier rail is carefully constructed around an aged kamahi tree), look across the deep river gorge where the rich, olive green of rimu stands out on the hillside, in contrast with the softer green of beech trees growing higher up on the drier ridgeline. Beech forest is the most widespread forest type in New Zealand, making up more than half of all our native forests. Podocarps are also a major component of New Zealand's forests and include some of our largest trees, such as rimu, kahikatea, miro, matai and totara.

Closer to the river, note the thriving kiekie, growing onto host trees or over the steep, moist banks. This climbing plant often reaches into the high tops of trees, attaching itself by aerial roots that cling to the trunks or find footing in tiny cracks, or it grows over rocks and fallen trees. It is a traditionally valuable plant for Maori weaving.

IN THE GORGE
From the lookout the track descends about 200 metres to the ❹ **flume bridge**. Cross this sturdy old concrete bridge over the flume pipe carrying water from the weir further up-river to the strainer house, which can now be seen over the river. Pause on the bridge to look into the shallow pools of the Hutt River. This is the start of the Hutt Gorge, popular with rafters and tyre tubers, but a trap for unwary river travellers who underestimate the distance and degree of wilderness involved in the journey from the Pakuratahi Forks to the next road-end at Te Marua. Such a trip can take

anything from three to six hours, depending on river flow.

Across the bridge, the ❺ **strainer house** and a sealed road seem a sudden and incongruous intrusion in the forest, but the road at least provides a top-quality walking track for the return part of this loop. An information panel on the strainer house provides details about the Kaitoke water catchment scheme.

Walk past the strainer house and onto the road, which heads uphill for the first 100 metres to a seat, then continues towards a huge, classic-shaped northern rata tree prominent beside the road. Its branches are laden with astelias and, if your walk is timed for December or January, chances are the tree will also be laden with blazing crimson flowers. The tin band circling its trunk was placed to protect the rata from possums; it's one of several rata along the roadway able to be accessed for this protection. Since attaching the tin, however, park management has carried out extensive possum control and all rata in the park – along with other plants that are favoured by possums – have flourished without the need for such protective measures.

After this short climb the walk is a delight, following the narrow, sealed road between mown, grassy edges and in a green corridor of towering podocarp trees. About 400 metres along this road Terrace Walk is signposted on the right. This is a 15-minute forest loop that has been built to a standard suitable for wheelchairs. Continue along the road or take a detour on this track, which has a few tree identification labels and which emerges back on the road about

PAKURATAHI RIVER WALK

Another walk, established a few years ago now, starts from near the park's camping area, crosses a bridge over the Pakuratahi River and meanders through impressive podocarp forest to the Pakuratahi Forks car park. Allow about 15 minutes each way. There is one very short zigzag climb but no steps on the track, which offers an alternative, off-road route to the Forks. To find the start, drive 400 m from the park entrance to a T-junction, turn right, then cross the bridge and drive to the Norman Kirk Memorial grove. The walk is signposted across and a few metres along the road from here.

300 metres further along. As you step out from the forest track, turn right and walk the final 200 metres along the road to complete this circuit. If you choose to stay on the road, you will pass two short, signposted river access tracks. Detour if you wish; though these are rougher and steeper than the road, the second track leads to a better swimming spot.

On the right just before the bridge over the Pakuratahi River is a ❻ **clearing** that was originally the site of caretakers' houses. The site underwent a major, though temporary, transformation to become 'Rivendell' during filming of the Lord of the Rings trilogy in 1999. Although nothing of this set remains, funds paid by the film company for the use of this site have been put towards development and maintenance of recreation facilities in the park, and the disappeared Rivendell today makes a delightful picnic spot.

A large rock before the bridge has a plaque with the curious inscription, 'Great things are done when man and mountains meet'. This was placed here to commemorate the construction of the water supply facilities, obviously by a man.

REFRESHMENTS

The Kaitoke Gardens and Café is on SH 2 about 1 km east of the park entrance, and Te Marua Store, also on SH 2, is 7 km towards Wellington. Picnic areas and coin-operated barbecues are available in the park. Bookings for large groups can be made with the ranger.

COLONIAL KNOB
Forest and fantastic views

START/FINISH
By Elsdon Youth Camp, Raiha Street, Porirua. Vehicle access is also via the Spicer Botanical Park carpark at the end of Broken Hill Road.

DISTANCE/TIME
9.5 km, 4–5 hours (loop)

ACCESS
By car, Raiha Street is at the junction of Main Road and Keneperu Drive between Tawa and Porirua. The walk starts 1.5 km along Raiha Street. By train, walk from Porirua station through North City Shopping Centre and across Raiha Walkway, starting on Titahi Bay Road and emerging on Raiha Street. Turn right to find the track entrance 300 m further on.

WHAT TO EXPECT UNDERFOOT Forest track, stepped and steep in parts, grassy track and four-wheel-drive road
DOGS No
MOUNTAIN BIKES No

This is just one of the many walks in the Wellington region that's within easy reach of the central city, yet traverses a mini wilderness of native forest and offers stunning outlooks. The summit (468 metres) is one of the highest points on the Wellington Peninsula. Pick your day and your climb to the top of Colonial Knob will reward with views that extend across mountains, forest parks, Cook Strait and the Marlborough Sound waterways.

The walk involves a reasonably challenging climb on hills that are fully exposed to the wild weather patterns that blast across Cook Strait. Even if it does seem calm and sunny at the carpark, take spare warm,

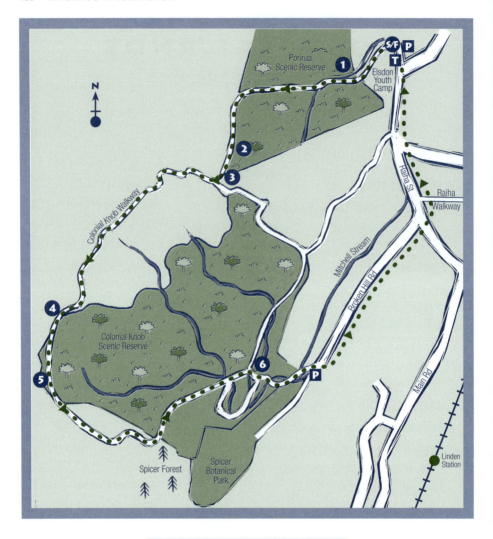

WALK KEY

❶ Kohekohe forest ❷ Open grassy area ❸ Stile ❹ Summit ridge
❺ Colonial Knob trig ❻ Number two reservoir

waterproof and windproof clothing with you.

This walk circuit passes through a mix of landscapes: the forest-filled stream gullies and hillsides of Porirua Scenic Reserve (managed by Porirua City Council), Colonial Knob Scenic Reserve (managed by the Department of Conservation) and private farmland. On the high points are communications masts and buildings, and a service road to these makes up part of this walking circuit.

Native forest on the walk includes pockets of mature tawa and kohekohe trees, which grow in the stream gullies, a few scattered podocarps, and secondary growth of regeneration-associated trees and shrubs such as rewarewa, mahoe, pukatea, nikau, kawakawa, hangehange, rangiora and tree ferns. The two reserves contain the largest remaining stand of native forest in the Porirua–Tawa region. The suburb of Tawa is named for the forest that once dominated the area. Of the native birdlife tui and fantail

RAIHA WALKWAY

This delightful trail links Porirua City and Porirua Scenic Reserve and provides significant enhancement to the former site of the Porirua Asylum. The Gothic-style stone asylum building was destroyed by an earthquake in 1942. Opened in 2000, the Raiha Walkway has been landscaped with boardwalks, bridges and wetland development and tree-planting help from local schoolchildren. Cabbage trees, flaxes, five finger, titoki and tawa are among the native plants now flourishing beside the trail. The 1.5 km walkway starts behind the North City Shopping Centre; it is signposted beside the corner of Hagley St and Titahi Bay Rd, and ends beside an industrial subdivision at 35 Raiha St, 300 m from Porirua Scenic Reserve and the Colonial Knob Track. Raiha Walkway also provides a link in the national walking trail Te Araroa (the Long Pathway).

are common, New Zealand pigeon are becoming more prolific and the rarer red-crowned parakeet and whitehead are sometimes seen here.

Kenepuru Hospital, located off Raiha Street, has been a key factor leading to the establishment of the two reserves. In 1894 much of the Colonial Knob land was set aside to secure an efficient water supply for the hospital. Two reservoirs were built in the headwaters of Mitchell Stream, and surrounding land was farmed for the hospital. The reservoirs became redundant when the hospital was connected to the main Porirua water supply, but they remained a focal point for swimming, picnics and forest walks. In 1976 the land was declared surplus to the hospital and the scenic reserve was established.

Porirua Scenic Reserve was formerly known as Prossers Bush, then Elsdon Scenic Reserve, and part of the land was set aside for 'scenic purposes' during subdivision development in Porirua in 1960. Colonial Knob Walkway was opened in 1973 as part of a proposed New Zealand-long walkway. On the same day another, distant link was opened on Mt Auckland, north of Auckland city.

The circuit described here involves a 2-kilometre walk along the road back to your starting point. There are other options for circuits which return more directly to your starting point, but the one described here gives the best look at both the views and the native forest in the two reserves. There is a third entrance on Raiha Street (see map).

Access over the private farmland is a privilege, so respect this and keep to the marked route.

THE WALK

The track that climbs through Porirua Scenic Reserve is clearly signposted at the carpark beside Elsdon Youth Camp. It enters the bush and climbs very gently through tall ❶ **kohekohe forest** beside a small stream. A couple of tracks join on the left from the youth camp.

After about 10 minutes a seat nestled beside a large pukatea tree provides a welcome rest spot. The climb continues, steepish in parts with steps and boardwalks along the way. As you walk note the variety of forest plants, each finding the growing conditions that suits it best. In the damp gully nikau palms flourish, while the drier banks beside the track are lined with understorey plants such as kawakawa, with its distinctive heart-shaped leaves, and rangiora.

About 50 minutes from the start you'll know the steepest climb of the circuit is over when the track breaks out of tall forest and leads through low-growing mahoe, hebe shrubs, rangiora, a touch of gorse, then an ❷ **open grassy area** to reach the reserve boundary. Tall rewarewa trees emerge above the low-growing canopy. Look back – you have earned some time to enjoy the view!

REWARD FOR THE CLIMB

About 250 metres from the bush edge the track crosses a ❸ **stile** and continues on private farmland. At this point you're about halfway to the trig. Forget the climb and enjoy the views! Turn right and follow the farm service road, signposted to Colonial Knob, which gradually climbs to the long summit ridge and then to the Colonial Knob trig point. (A left turn at this junction leads down the road and through a long, farmed gully to the second Raiha Street entrance.)

Follow the walkway markers along the ❹ **summit ridge**, stick to the track and enjoy the views. To the north are the twin harbours of Porirua and Pauatahanui. Legendary Polynesian explorer Kupe is said to have named Porirua as a reference to the 'two flowings of the tide'. These sheltered inlets, with their good food sources and handy access to coastal fishing grounds, were among the first areas settled in the greater Wellington region. Like the Marlborough Sounds, which can be seen across Cook Strait, the two harbours are, in fact, drowned river valleys.

Just offshore, guarding the entrance to Porirua and Pauatahanui, is Mana Island. This island was once farmed but is now a valuable wildlife sanctuary that offers a safe, predator-free habitat for several threatened native species, including takahe and the re-establishment of several seabird species. Further north is Kapiti Island, a predator-free reserve that is one of the largest islands in the world to have its rat population totally eradicated. (See page 153 for a guide to walking Kapiti Island.)

The craggy, sometimes snow-covered ranges of Tararua Forest Park lie to the north-east and, if the day is really clear, you might see the symmetrical

PATAKA MUSEUM AND GALLERY

Cnr Norrie and Parumoana Sts, Porirua City
Open Monday–Saturday 10 am–4.30 pm,
Sunday 11 am–4.30 pm
Admission free
Pataka showcases contemporary New Zealand and Pacific art and presents histories that reflect the many cultures of Porirua. Pataka incorporates the Whitireia Performing Arts School, Kaizen Café, a Japanese garden created with help from Porirua's Japanese sister city Misio, and the city library.

cone of Mt Taranaki (Mt Egmont) in the distance. To the south views extend, ridgeline after ridgeline, over the closer hills of Karori and Makara and beyond to the Marlborough Sounds and Kaikoura mountains.

SUMMIT, SIGNAL MASTS AND STILES

The scattered native vegetation along the ridge is described as a 'cloud forest community', and it is affected by the severe climatic conditions of this exposed spot. It has been modified by fire but is now regenerating well. Colonial Knob and other hills of similar height across this northern Wellington region, such as Boulder Hill in Belmont Regional Park, are the few surviving remnants of an old peneplain, an eroded land mass uplifted by earthquake then cut and dissected by erosion.

About 20 to 30 minutes' walk along this top section of walkway will take you past a conglomeration of communications masts and buildings (look for the large blue picnic tables and seats about 70m to the left of the ridge line track) and eventually to the ❺ Colonial Knob trig. Past the trig, cross a stile that leads back into private farm land, then look for marker poles across open paddocks as you descend towards the forest edge of Colonial Knob Scenic Reserve.

The view now looks over the suburbs of Linden and Tawa and the hills of Belmont Regional Park. (You may wish to disregard the less attractive closer outlook of Porirua's Spicer Landfill and its hundreds of wheeling black-backed gulls!)

Close to the forest edge, just to the south, marker posts can be seen emerging from the pine trees of Spicer Forest. These mark the Wellington section of Te Araroa (the Long Pathway), which connects Wellington city with Porirua via the Northern Walkway, Ohariu Valley, Spicer Forest and Colonial Knob.

After about 800 metres from the trig the track returns once more from private farmland into the scenic reserve. Pine trees and scattered gorse soon give way to tall native forest; look for rimu and rata standing tall amongst the more dominant mahoe, broadleaf, five finger, young kohekohe and mapou. Rata vines cover the trunks of many of the tall trees.

THE RESERVOIR THAT ISN'T

The forest track descends to a major junction. A sign here indicates 'Number one reservoir' to the right and 'Number two reservoir and Elsdon carpark' straight ahead. The number one reservoir was drained following serious erosion in the early 1900s and there is nothing to see but a grassy basin, so continue straight ahead towards the ❻ **number two reservoir**.

Follow the track as it climbs over a forested ridge for about 100 metres then descends gradually to the reservoir and a second track junction. The left-hand option climbs to the southern boundary of Colonial Knob reserve then descends to Raiha Street. Our route takes us to the right, but first cross the little bridge that leads to a grassy clearing overlooking the pretty little reservoir nestled in its forested basin. Rewarewa trees stand out, high above other native trees and shrubs.

Return to the track, which descends first beside an old tailrace then crosses the stream and about 100 metres from the reservoir arrives at the bush edge and boundary with Spicer Park.

Follow the track which leads into the park and turn left, wandering through open grassy clearings interspersed with plantings of exotic trees, to arrive at the carpark located at the end of Broken Hill Road.

To complete the loop, walk 1 kilometre to the start of Broken Hill Road then turn left and walk a further 1 kilometre along Raiha Street to your starting point.

REFRESHMENTS

North City Shopping Centre in Porirua features an extensive food hall and is open seven days a week. Other cafés and hotels in the city include Kaizen licensed café at Pataka Museum and Gallery.

WAIRAKA POINT
A coastal journey

START
Pukerua Bay waterfront

FINISH
Plimmerton village

DISTANCE/TIME
8 km, 3–4 hours (one-way); 12 km if walking between Pukerua Bay and Plimmerton railway stations

ACCESS
A two-car drop-off is one option to do this walk. Leave one car at Plimmerton village, then drive to the far end of Pukerua Bay on SH 1. As SH 1 turns right, veer left onto Pukerua Beach Road and descend to Ocean Parade. Turn left. The walk starts 800 m from here.
By train, get off at Pukerua Bay station, walk along Te Motu Road and cross SH 1 via the footbridge, then walk north on SH 1 to Ocean Beach Road. Part way down this road take a footpath to the beach and Ocean Parade. Turn left and walk 400 m to the road-end. (Muri station is closer, but involves crossing busy SH 1 with no overbridge.)

WHAT TO EXPECT UNDERFOOT Narrow, rocky, dirt track, stony beach, quarry road, no hills
DOGS Must be on a leash (safeguarding the little blue penguins)
MOUNTAIN BIKES Yes

WAIRAKA POINT 137

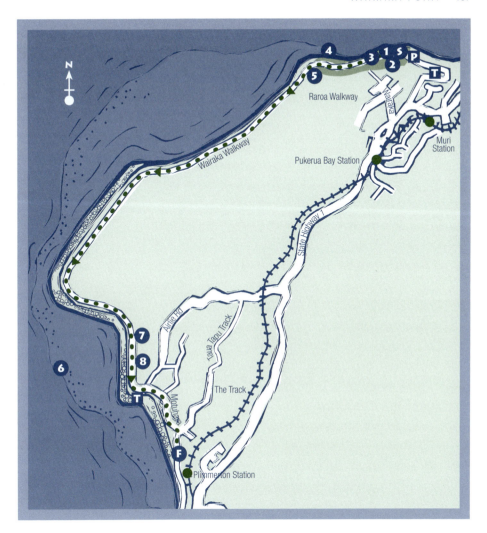

WALK KEY

❶ Wairaka Wildlife Reserve ❷ Grove of karaka trees ❸ Rock arch
❹ Wairaka Point ❺ Grassy clearing ❻ Tokaapapa (Grandfather Reef)
❼ Old quarry buildings ❽ Hongoeka marae

This long coastal walk, known well by local residents, gives a rather different perspective of the journey from Pukerua Bay to Plimmerton than the frenetic SH 1 option. Probably the best feature of this walk is the constant presence of a great coastal outlook. Kapiti Island nestles offshore just 15 kilometres to the north and, on clear days, the gentle hills of the Marlborough Sounds will look close enough to touch.

Pukerua Bay (Pukerua means two hills) was a strategic point on the early Maori coastal route for its proximity to the South Island and Kapiti Island. Ngati Tara (then Ngati Ira) lived here, until Ngati Toa arrived in the region in the early 1800s. The development of major transport links – the railway in 1888 and main road in 1939 – forever changed the nature of the formerly quiet farming and seaside village. Many residents now commute daily to work in Wellington city.

Despite the proximity to the northern satellite populations of Pukerua Bay and Plimmerton there is a strong feeling of remoteness on this rocky shoreline, which is isolated by huge, towering cliffs. A variety of native wildlife lives in this harsh coastal environment. Little blue penguins nest in the coastal scrub, shags, terns, white-faced herons, gulls and kingfishers fish just offshore, and several species of geckos and skinks live under boulders and in the scrub.

Obviously this walk can be tackled in either direction. This description heads southwards; some say the track tends to be less exposed this way but a bitter southerly would easily prove that theory wrong. Head south anyway,

> **RAROA WALKWAY**
>
> This short walk has a stunning outlook on the cliff tops above Pukerua Bay. A gentle 10-minute climb will take you through kohekohe forest to the cliff edge, where you can look down onto the rocky coastline of the Wairaka Point walk, across to Kapiti Island and, if the day is clear, as far the Kaikoura mountains and Mt Taranaki (also known as Mt Egmont).
>
> Turn off SH 1 onto Wairaka Rd, travel 300 m to the end, turn left (into Raroa Place) and drive 50 m to the road end. An access track signposted Raroa Reserve leads between houses, then along a fence line and through forest to the cliff-top lookout point.

if for no other reason than to enjoy a well-earned rest in a Plimmerton café at the completion of your walk.

The first part of the walk passes through a Department of Conservation reserve, while at the Plimmerton end public access follows an old quarry road. The *Porirua City Heritage Trail* brochure, available from the Porirua City Council, provides historic information about this area.

Note: if the tide is high and a strong westerly wind is blowing, access around Wairaka Point can be difficult. It is possible to clamber over, but if in doubt check the tide times and time your walk to avoid high tide.

THE WALK

From the end of Ocean Beach Road walk along the small terrace above a rocky tidal platform for 50 metres to the ❶ **Wairaka Wildlife Reserve**, then follow the obvious track along the back of the rocky beach. The scientific reserve is home to several skinks and geckos, including the endangered Whitaker's skink. Pukerua Bay is one of only three places, and the only known mainland habitat, where this skink is found. Other Whitaker's skink colonies are found on the Mercury Islands off Coromandel Peninsula. At 20 centimetres in length it is one of the larger lizard species, but chances of seeing one at Pukerua Bay are slim. It is nocturnal and hides by day among the shrub-covered boulders and scree. Control of rodents and mustelids (ferrets, stoats and weasels) has helped rid the reserve of predator threats to the skinks and geckos.

Continue along the coast, walking through the hardy native shrubs that survive in this wind-swept, salty environment. Matted *Muehlenbeckia complexa* (pohuehue) is also known as wire vine for its tangled, wiry stems; this common coastal groundcover often climbs over rocks, sand dunes and other plants.

Cassinia, or tauhinu, has a common English name of cottonwood because of the fine white hairs that cover the leaves and branches. Its growth is so prolific around the coastal hills of Wellington it is considered a nuisance to farmers and for some years was declared a noxious weed – a designation since revoked!

A tiny ❷ **grove of karaka trees** stands out above the low-growing shrubs near the base of the cliffs. Karaka was such an important tree for early Maori for food and medicinal use that it was deliberately planted in many dwelling sites. Several other native plants that survive on this little piece of coastline, though more obscure to the average beach walker with no special botanical knowledge, are now considered rare in other parts of Wellington.

ROCKY OUTCROPS

A 10-metre-high ❸ **rock arch** is prominent about 100 metres along the beach. From there, continue to pick your way along the narrow foot track, through the shrubs and over and around rocks just above the beach, until you come to ❹ **Wairaka Point**. Wairaka was the name of the wife of Hau, an East Coast chief from Mahia Peninsula. Legend tells that Wairaka fled from Mahia and reached this coast before being caught by Hau and turned into rock.

There are several rocky outcrops to clamber over at the point, and around the corner a little cave to explore and perhaps seek refuge in should a strong northerly prevail. If the tide is particularly high you might need to clamber over the rocks to get around the point.

Having safely negotiated the point enjoy the new outlook beyond the long expanse of the shingle beach to Porirua Harbour entrance and the headland of Whitireia.

Walk a few minutes from the point to a little ❺ **grassy clearing** and stream, which is an oasis on this remote and stark coastline. The clearing was once the site of Nobby Clarke's cottage, the home of the man known as the hermit of Pukerua Bay. Today it makes a great picnic spot.

The next 3 kilometres of your walk stretch ahead of you, a wide, curved beach covered with stones and driftwood. Behind, the cliffs rise steeply, some 150 metres high and covered with grass and coastal shrubbery. Pick your way across the shingle; if this becomes too tiring climb onto the grassy terraces along the back of the beach, where the going is easier. Note how sharply the beach falls off, in case you're tempted to take a swim.

TAUA TAPU TRACK

On the hill behind Plimmerton is Taua Tapu Track, part of a historic foot trail to Pukerua Bay. It takes about 30 minutes to walk and has great views. It extends from the track (which leads off Motuhara Road, Plimmerton) to Airlie Road (which crosses from Moana Road, on the Plimmerton waterfront, to SH 1). This track crosses private farmland, so please respect the privilege. No dogs during lambing (August 1 to September 30).

At the far, southern end of the beach, you can choose to continue clambering around the rocks, or climb off the beach a little to an old quarry road. The easier travel along the road may make a welcome change after clambering over the stony beach.

REEFS AND INLETS

The road follows the coastline of Hongoeka Bay. Depending on the tide, the reef known as ❻ **Tokaapapa (Grandfather Reef)** may be exposed just offshore. Across the bay is Ngati Toa Domain, the entrance to Porirua and Pauatahanui inlets and the oldest settlement site in the Wellington region. Known also as Paremata, and now Mana, this area was said to have been visited by famous Polynesian explorer Kupe and to have been occupied permanently since about AD 1450.

Shortly after the road passes by the former ❼ **Plimmerton quarry buildings** it arrives at ❽ **Hongoeka marae**, which has been a Ngati Toa village since the 1820s. This region was a stronghold of the Ngati Ira tribe until they were displaced by the Ngati Toa tribe, who arrived here under the leadership of the chief Te Rauparaha in the early 1800s.

The access road to and beyond the marae are private, but the public are welcome to walk along it to reach the end of Moana Road and the Plimmerton waterfront. From here you can enjoy the 2.5-kilometre wander along the waterfront, onto Sunset Road and around the point to Plimmerton village and railway station. This route takes you beside Karehana Bay, which is likely to be dotted with windsurfers, then around the point to Beach Road and Plimmerton village. The point, now the site of the Plimmerton fire station, was once the fortified pa site of Te Rauparaha's nephew, Te Rangihaeata. Te Rauparaha himself lived at Taupo village at the southern end of Plimmerton beach.

REFRESHMENTS

Plimmerton's generous choice of cafés and takeaway outlets are deservedly popular. Take time at the end of your walk to sample some of their fare.

BATTLE HILL
Farm, forest and a battle story

START/FINISH
Battle Hill Farm Forest Park, Paekakariki Hill Road

DISTANCE/TIME
3 km, 1.5 hours (loop)

ACCESS
Battle Hill is on the Paekakariki Hill Road 10 km from Paekakariki and 6 km from Pauatahanui. From SH 1 turn east at Paremata onto SH 58, drive 5 km around the inlet to Pauatahanui and continue straight ahead onto Paekakariki Hill Road. Alternatively, turn onto Grays Road at Plimmerton and drive around the northern shore of the inlet then turn left onto Paekakariki Hill Road. The park is clearly signposted on the eastern side of the road.

WHAT TO EXPECT UNDERFOOT Shingle, dirt and grass track. A few steps
DOGS No. Battle Hill is a farm – no dogs are allowed, not even shut in vehicles
MOUNTAIN BIKES Yes, on the farmland but not in the bush reserve

This walk in the multi-use Battle Hill Farm Forest Park offers a mix of experiences: native forest, farmland, rural views, great picnic spots – and information displays about farming and the history of the park.

The 500-hectare park in the Horokiri valley has been developed by the regional council for farming, forestry and recreational use. In the front paddocks there are grassy, shaded areas set aside for picnicking and camping, with fireplaces, toilets – and safe swimming or paddling opportunities for young children in the Horokiri Stream (west branch).

The headwaters of this stream flow through the park's bush reserve, where 40 hectares of

BATTLE HILL 143

WALK KEY

1. Abbotts Field
2. Battle Hill information panel
3. Summit
4. Kohekohe trees
5. Grassy clearing
6. Corner Paddock

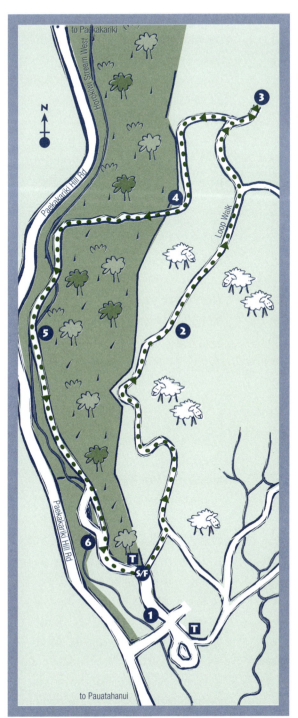

kohekohe and tawa forest are fenced and protected. The rest of the park is devoted to farming or commercial forestry activities, where roads and tracks are also available for mountain biking, horse riding and for longer walks than the one described.

Because Battle Hill is a working farm, management asks that walkers use stiles and gates, and leave all gates as found, open or closed.

THE WALK

From the park entrance continue 100 metres to a small barn on the left. Turn left just past the barn into ❶ **Abbotts Field**, which is a popular park camping and picnic area. The walk starts about 200 metres from the Abbots Paddock entrance. You can park anywhere – there is plenty of room.

The walk can be tackled in either direction; this description heads to the right, climbs through the open paddocks to the summit and then descends through the bush.

Follow the road through the paddock, until about 50 metres before the toilets where a major information sign indicates the start of the walk to Battle Hill. Head up the grassy track for 50 metres, go through a gate and continue upwards on a farm road and then into open country, following the signs to Battle Hill.

The track winds its way uphill on a steepish grade and the view expands as you climb, becoming a multi-green coloured mosaic of pine forest, farm paddocks, hillsides and gullies of regenerating native forest.

About 30 to 40 minutes from the start of the walk an ❷ **information panel** on the ridge marks the site where Ngati Toa chief Te Rangihaeata made his stand in 1846. This incident represents a significant chapter in the history of settlement in the region.

HISTORIC STAND

Along with his famous uncle Te Rauparaha, Te Rangihaeata had disputed a number of land settlements. As a result, Te Rauparaha was arrested at his pa at Plimmerton and troops set out to find his 'troublesome' nephew. Te Rangihaeata, whose pa was then at Pauatahanui, retreated to this strategic location in Horokiri valley.

In those days the valley was filled with thick native forest and the British troops slogged through heavy rain for two days in pursuit. When they arrived one witness was moved to write of Te Rangihaeata's defensive position, 'No position could have been better chosen or more unassailable.' After trying with little effect to close in on Te Rangihaeata, the British started shelling with mortars. By the end of a week-long siege eight men had been killed, some from each side, but Te Rangihaeata eventually escaped.

The information panel provides an excellent first-hand description of events during the siege. With a little imagination one can visualise the desperate scenes as they unfolded one rainy August more than 150 years ago.

To continue, climb about 200 metres along the ridge to a seat, then a junction. Veer left and walk to a second junction, meeting with a track that has climbed through the bush reserve.

There is more information here relating to the history of Battle Hill.

The final 100-metre climb to the ❸ summit is a steep grunt, but well worth the effort. Once there, take a break on the welcome seat and enjoy the view down Horokiri valley towards Pauatahanui, with Transmission Gully on your left. The carved rock on the summit was placed there in 1996 by the Wellington Regional Council and Ngati Toa iwi to commemorate the 150th anniversary of the battle.

PAUATAHANUI INLET

This inlet is the only large estuarine wetland left in the lower North Island. Although much of the inlet has been modified and drained, over 40 hectares of salt marsh at the eastern end is designated as a wildlife reserve and managed jointly by the Department of Conservation and Royal Forest and Bird Protection Society. Since 1984 the society has been working to restore the wetland with an extensive replanting programme to improve the habitat for wading birds. More than 20 resident and migratory bird species are commonly seen on the reserve.

Public paths and boardwalks suitable for wheelchairs have been built on the reserve and hides have been placed at strategic locations. The best viewing time is at high tide, when birds come in from the inlet. Some overseas migratory birds stay here throughout summer, and ducks breed here in June and July.

The entrance to the reserve is by the community hall in Pauatahanui village. Nature trail guides are available and contributions to the donation box are welcome!

FROM BATTLE TO BUSH
To complete your circuit retrace your steps from the summit, head right at the sign that says 'Loop track' and descend through the farm paddock to a dirt track that meets the fenceline. The fence protects the regenerating trees and shrubs in the reserve from grazing by stock. Follow the track markers past gorse and native tauhinu (cassinia) on the left and the forest-filled Horokiri valley on the right.

The descent continues around the side of the hill (you may need to rock hop through a boggy patch), looking down to the bright green tops of mahoe and broadleaf trees at the head of the valley, and then the track enters the native forest.

Look for the young rata growing alongside the track before it descends into the shade of some very big ❹ **kohekohe trees**. Although this frost-tender tree is common around the Wellington region, it is now far less widespread than it once was. Note how the close-knit canopy of leaves blocks light and prevents much growth on the forest floor. This is typical of kohekohe, which is the only species in New Zealand of the tropical mahogany family.

The forest changes as you wander along the valley. Big tawa trees become dominant, towering over a profusion of understorey plants such as mahoe, hangehange, kawakawa and tree ferns. The branches of some especially big tawa are laden with clumps of epiphytic astelias.

The track follows Horokiri Stream and comes to a ❺ **grassy clearing**, a lovely picnic spot surrounded by tall tawa, rewarewa and mahoe trees. Cross the wooden bridge and walk another 70 metres or so to a second, smaller clearing, cross a second bridge and follow the stream.

Near the end of the track there is a junction; the right-hand fork is signposted 'Corner Paddock'. Please yourself which way you go – you are now on the park's 'Forest Loop Walk' and after about 150 metres both tracks arrive at different corners of ❻ **Corner Paddock**, about 200 metres from your starting point.

REFRESHMENTS
At Battle Hill people are welcome to bring their own barbecues. Pauatahanui village has a café/restaurant, a dairy that dispenses very generous ice creams, and a boutique movie theatre with it's own café.

QUEEN ELIZABETH PARK
Walking in the dunelands

START/FINISH
Queen Elizabeth Park, between Paekakariki and Raumati (MacKays Crossing entrance)

DISTANCE/TIME
6.5 km, 2-3 hours (loop)

ACCESS
By car, drive 45 km north of Wellington on SH 1 and turn into the park entrance at MacKays Crossing. Continue along the park road (Whareroa Road) for 1.7 km, turn left at an intersection and drive 200 m to the road-end and carpark.
By train, travel to Paekakariki then walk 1.5 km (via Robertson and Wellington Roads) to the southern park entrance. You will need to join the walk circuit at its southern point.

WHAT TO EXPECT UNDERFOOT Grass and metal, gently undulating track, some sealed road; beach walking optional
DOGS Yes (not permitted on farmland or wetlands; you'll see lots on other tracks)
MOUNTAIN BIKES Yes

This walk follows a figure-of-eight circuit along the coastline and inland dunes of Queen Elizabeth Park. The key attractions of the walk are wandering among the dunes through stands of low-growing native coastal shrubs and alongside the often wild beach that extends along the length of the park, with the constant view of sentinel-like Kapiti Island. Seabirds, pukeko, welcome swallows and fantails are the birds likely to make their presence known along the way, and in summer look for tui feeding on flax flowers.

There seems to be so much going on at this park – picnic areas, horse riding, dog walking, tram rides, a model aeroplane club, a surf club, children's play areas, a holiday park

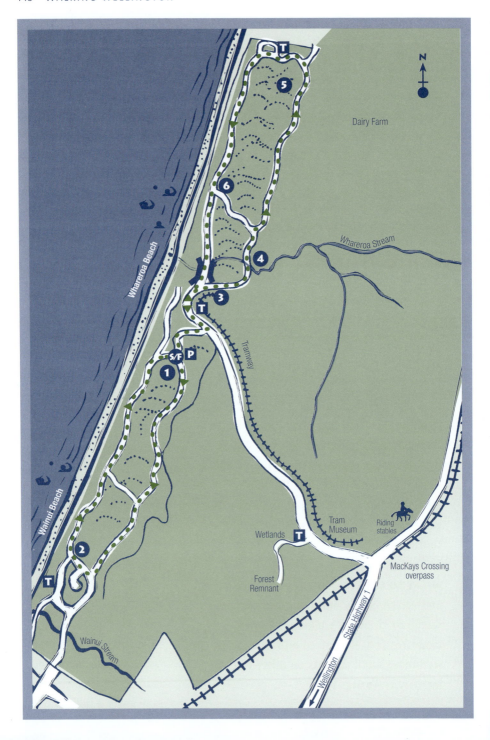

WALK KEY

① Seat and view point
② Picnic areas
③ Model aeroplane club
④ Bridge
⑤ Mature coastal forest
⑥ Side track to inland coastal track

and a substantial farming operation – that it's a pleasant surprise to discover a feeling of wild remoteness among the coastal dunelands. And the ever-growing population spreading along the Kapiti Coast makes this rare expanse of uninhabited beach and dunes even more significant.

The dunes are a special environment, ever shifting, ever changing, reliant on sand-binding vegetation for stability. The gullies and hills of the dunes are covered with such hardy plants as flax, bracken, creeping muehlenbeckia (pohuehue), tauhinu (cottonwood), spinifex (sand grass), broadleaf, taupata (*Coprosma repens*) and other coprosma shrubs that can withstand the constant onslaught of salt winds. Local environmental groups have helped regional council efforts to enhance this native plant cover, with major revegetation work and by eradicating weeds such as pampas grass.

The abundance of seafood along this coastline made the area appealing to early Maori people. Pa sites are located on two larger sandhills, and middens (rubbish piles) of shells are common throughout the dunes. In more recent times, a flurry of human activity occurred here during World War II, when 20,000 United States marines were based in three camps in the area. Their presence is marked by the memorial gates at the MacKays Crossing park entrance and an

KAPITI COAST ELECTRIC TRAMWAY

Open weekends, public and summer holidays 11 am–4.30 pm
Phone 0-4-292 8361
www.wellingtontrams.org.nz
Take a ride through the park on a restored street tram, one that operated in Wellington city in the early 1900s. The tram leaves from the Wellington Tramway Museum, just inside the MacKays Crossing park entrance, where old trams, photographs and memorabilia are displayed. Tram rides travel on a line through the park to Whareroa Beach.

interpretative display on Whareroa Road, the site of one of the camps.

Queen Elizabeth Park is managed by the Greater Wellington Regional Council. As well as the tracks described here, several other tracks wind in and out of the dunes and onto the beach. There are two major picnic areas in the park, at the end of Whareroa Road (via MacKays Crossing entrance) and at Wainui Beach, at the southern, Paekakariki end.

THE WALK

From the carpark follow the sealed road southwards through the vehicle barrier. After 100 metres our route, the Paekakariki Inland Track, is signposted; the wide track, sealed at first then a mix of grass and metal, undulates along the crest of the inland dunes about 300 metres in from the beach.

Vegetation is sparse at first: look for the vine-like, tiny-leaved muehlenbeckia (pohuehue) tangled among bracken fern. As you progress the coastal shrublands thicken, particularly in sheltered gullies and on the lee side of the dunes, where mahoe, flax and several coprosma species grow in healthy profusion.

As you walk over the higher dunes, your views will take in much of the 638-hectare Queen Elizabeth Park. Looking inland, the grazed farmland of the park is a contrast to the shrub-covered dunes.

KAPITI ISLAND TO THE KAIKOURA MOUNTAINS

Continuing along the track, take advantage of the seaward outlook from a ❶ **track-side seat**. It extends north to Waikanae and south to Pukerua Bay, with Mana Island beyond and, weather permitting, as far as the Marlborough Sounds and Kaikoura mountains. Looking closer, Kapiti Island rises from the sea just 6 kilometres offshore. The gentle contours of this visible eastern side of the island wildlife sanctuary are a contrast to those out of sight on the far, western side, where sheer cliffs plunge vertically from the island's highest point into the sea.

Continue southwards. From here on, several side-tracks cross the main trail, many heading towards the sea, but to follow this circuit continue to the sealed park road at the southern, Paekakariki end of the park. This was the site of one of the US military camps; today the scene is one of secluded and sheltered ❷ **picnic areas** hidden away behind coastal shrubs. There is also a holiday park, a surf club and a children's play area here, but this walk circuit bypasses such 'civilisation'.

When you reach the sealed road,

FOREST AND WETLANDS

Between the dunes and the park's boundary with SH 1, a small patch of tall forest stands like an island in the farmland. This is a tiny but significant remnant of the kohekohe and kahikatea forest that once covered these coastal plains. Karaka and rewarewa also grow in this patch, which is fenced to prevent farm stock trampling and grazing on young seedlings. Unseen from the track, lying low beside the forest, is another significant natural area in the park, about 10 ha of wetlands that are home to wetland birds and some regionally rare plants.

A track starts from behind the World War II display, crosses the equestrian events area and leads to the wetlands then on across farmland to the forest remnant.

turn right and walk towards the sea, then turn right at a T-junction and walk 175 metres to the road-end and signposted start of the Coastal Track. If you travel to the park by train, this is where you can pick up this circuit. The Coastal Track returns to the Whareroa carpark, passing through patches of native shrubs and two large grassy areas. The long expanse of sandy beach lies close to the track, so if you want a change underfoot hop across and travel along the sand.

To complete the first part of this figure-of-eight circuit, the Coastal Track climbs gently for 100 metres and returns to the carpark. The second part of the walk travels the park's northern coastline in a similar way – out along an inland dune track and back along the coast.

THE NORTHERN DUNES

From the carpark head back to Whareroa Road, turn left and follow the road as it curves to the right and ends in a smaller carpark. By the end of the tramline diagonally cross a grassy paddock, heading inland, and you will pick up the start of the track. (If you've been walking along the beach, turn inland when you come to the Whareroa Stream outlet; the tramline and grassy paddock will be about 150 metres inland on your right.)

The Inland Track follows the line between dunes and farmland about 500 metres inland from the sea. The only reminder that a major city exists just 45 kilometres down the road is the distant roar of SH 1 traffic. Soon after the start the grassy track passes behind the park's ❸ **model aeroplane club** and heads between the sandhills in the direction of the sea, past a sign pointing to Whareroa Stream. After crossing a ❹ **bridge** over Whareroa Stream the track branches right, turns back inland and wends its way behind the dunes.

Quite a lot of blackberry grows near the start of the track, but further along a significant stand of ❺ **mature coastal forest** covers the northernmost dunes. Geologists rate these northern dunes as the only totally unmodified dunes in the region.

At the far, northern end of the park, the Inland Track veers left away from the fenceline (where a track signposted to Rainbow Court continues straight ahead), climbs over a dune and descends to the northern, Raumati park entrance. Your coastal return track is obvious – a wide metal road that climbs onto the grass – and shrub-covered dunes. It then becomes a more narrow, grassy and dirt track as it undulates its way southwards, dropping close to the beach at times. A fence protects the revegetated dunes, nevertheless there are several beach access tracks along the way.

Again, feel free to wander the beach instead of the track. Just remember to turn inland by Whareroa Stream if you are returning to your parked car.

Soon after passing a ❻ **side-track** (this leads through to the Inland Track) the track enters one of the park's picnic areas, then comes to a wide wooden bridge that crosses Whareroa Stream as it winds to the beach on an ever-changing course through the ever-changing dunes. Walk up the road from the bridge for another 50 metres to the end of Whareroa Road to complete your figure of eight.

> **REFRESHMENTS**
>
> Have a picnic by the beach! There are 14 designated picnic areas at Wainui and Whareroa beaches, each with barbecue pads (BYO barbecue) and landscaped with shrubs to provide shelter and privacy. The park can be very busy, particularly during summer, and these areas can be reserved. When it's open the tramway museum also sells drinks and ice creams. Alternatively, try the cafés at Paekakariki or those on Rosetta Road, Raumati.

KAPITI ISLAND
Walking with the birds

START/FINISH
Kapiti Boat Club, Paraparaumu Beach (for boat access to the island)

DISTANCE/TIME
Rangatira Point 3–4 hours, 8 km
North End 2–3 hours, 5 km
Take your time on these walks to see the birds

ACCESS
Paraparaumu Beach is 3.5 km from the town centre and SH 1, and about 1 hour's drive from Wellington. Two DOC-licensed operators provide daily boat services (weather dependent) for passengers with DOC permits. Permits can be obtained on line at www.doc.govt.nz or at the DOC Visitor Centre, Manners St, Wellington, phone 0-4-384 7770 or email wellingtonvc@doc.govt.nz. Permits cost $11 (adult) and $5 (child), and boat fares are approximately $55 (adult) and $30 (child). Fifty permits are allocated per day for Rangatira Point and eighteen for North End.
Private boats are not permitted.
If trips are cancelled because of weather or sea conditions, permits and bookings can be transferred to another date.

WHAT TO EXPECT UNDERFOOT Well graded shingle and earthen tracks, some steps. A mix of gentle climbing and flat walking
DOGS Must be on a leash

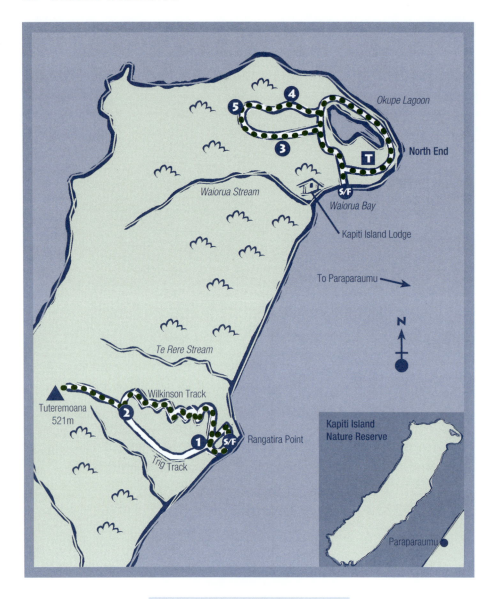

WALK KEY

❶ Whare ❷ Stitchbird feeder ❸ Southern loop track
❹ Northern loop track ❺ Viewpoint

It takes a little effort to get there, but the boat trip, the bird life, the bush and delightful island walks make a visit to Kapiti a truly memorable experience.

One of New Zealand's most significant nature reserves and successful conservation stories, Kapiti was one of the first islands of its size in the world to have all animal predators removed.

Following a history of Maori settlement, whaling, deforestation and farming, Kapiti was declared a 'public reserve' over one hundred years ago, following the urging of far-sighted conservationists who even then could see its ark-like potential. The forest recovery, predator control and successful releases of endangered species since have been at the forefront of international conservation achievement.

In the early 1900s a few little spotted kiwi, their species at risk because of forest destruction and introduced animal predators, were released on Kapiti. Soon after, they became extinct on the mainland – for over a hundred years, in fact, until 20 birds were re-located from Kapiti to Karori Sanctuary in 2000. In more recent years other successful transfers to Kapiti, following its predator-free status, have included kokako, stitchbird, kaka, whitehead, saddleback and takahe, along with a number of reptiles and invertebrates.

KAPITI MARINE RESERVE

Your boat trip to Kapiti Island passes through one of the first marine reserves created in New Zealand. Marine scientists have recorded significant increases in the sizes and numbers of fish and shellfish since 1992, when the reserve was established. Beneath the surface, divers report the existence of some of the finest underwater scenery in the Wellington region: distinctive bouldery, sandy and sheltered reef habitats that provide a home to a variety of sponges, seaweed beds, starfish, corals, shellfish and fish. They also report that since the reserve was created fish and crayfish have become quite tame in the presence of divers.

On the surface, dolphins, orca and whales are occasional visitors, seals come and go from the small colonies on Kapiti Island, and seabirds are prolific. Keep an eye open for Australasian gannet/takapu, blue penguin/korora, sooty shearwater/titi, shags, gulls and terns.

While the island now offers safe refuge for some of New Zealand's rarest birds, it is also one of the few highly protected nature reserves open to public access. Accordingly there are some restrictions and conditions placed on public visitation.

Nevertheless, visiting Kapiti is not difficult – all it takes is a little pre-planning: getting a permit from the Department of Conservation, booking boat transport with one of the two DOC-licensed operators, packing a lunch, driving to Paraparaumu Beach to board the boat, checking your bag for unwanted rodent stowaways, and after just a 20-minute crossing you'll be on the island, probably besieged by screeching kaka, walking among ground-feeding takahe and kereru, and listening to a cacophony of tui, bellbirds, parakeets, and others.

Permit spaces fill quickly during summer and public holidays so it pays to book ahead for those times. However a trip can be made any time of the year. Interestingly, the weather can be more settled in winter and the birds are generally more active in autumn and winter.

Boat schedules allow around 6 hours on the island, plenty of time to explore and enjoy the walks. Facilities on the island include public shelters, toilets and walking tracks. There are no shops or cafes, so you will need to pack a picnic. (Overnight stays are an option at Kapiti Island Lodge, but they must be pre-booked.)

THE WALK

There are two landing areas, Rangatira Point and North End. You will need to choose one or the other when getting your permit from DOC – there is no access between the two. Each offers excellent walking options, great views and lots of birds for company.

At both landing points, on arrival there is a compulsory introductory talk by a DOC-contracted guide, covering track conditions, safety and special precautions to safeguard the special environment and wildlife, as well as information on Kapiti and its natural and human history. This talk significantly enhances any visitor's experience to the area.

One firm message you will be given is not to feed the birds; they need to rely on natural food from the forest and not become dependent on picnic-carrying visitors. This might be easier said than done, however, especially when boisterous kaka or sneaky weka spot potential supermarket snacks. I recall the look of distress on my young daughter's face when a speedy kaka quickly claimed her accidentally dropped chocolate chippie biscuit!

RANGATIRA POINT

The key features here are Rangatira Flat, an open grassy and wetland area, and Wilkinson Track, which leads through the forest to the island's summit. While most visitors here head straight for the summit, the secret is to take your time, make the journey the thing, in which case you are likely to see more birds along the way.

As you disembark from your launch you will be directed to the public shelter for the introductory talk. Step up from the beach and head to your right, following a wide grassy track along Rangatira Flat for about 5 minutes to the shelter. Note the old whaling pot by the shelter, left from the island's whaling station days.

Following the talk, wander an inland track along Rangatira Flat, where you are likely to be joined by resident weka and takahe, into the forest and up a gentle, 50-metre track to the ❶ **historic whare**. Originally built in the 1860s as a farm cottage, the whare went on to become the home of island caretakers, including the very famous early conservationist Richard Henry. Since 1924 it has acted as a temporary base for a succession of scientists, trappers and conservation staff.

Listen here for the quiet chatter of whiteheads in treetops, and enjoy the likely photograph opportunities of the more obvious, in-your-face kaka.

Wilkinson Track heads uphill from the whare. It is a high quality track that climbs on a gentle grade through subtly changing forest, ranging from regenerating kanuka to more mature podocarp forest closer to the top.

There are seats along the way; good spots to pause and let the birds come to you. Tui, bellbird and possibly the aptly named saddleback will be present, and North Island robin likely to be hopping curiously around your feet. On the downhill side of the junction with Trig Track, take a rest beside the small ❷ **bird feeder** on the left of the track. This provides supplementary food while the forest completes its regeneration process, and is particularly popular with stitchbirds. Wait around if there's no bird present when you arrive; chances are one is not far away.

On the summit, Tuteremoana (521 m), there is a small clearing – a great lunch spot – and a dramatic outlook over the very rugged western coast of Kapiti Island; the steep cliffs here contrast with the more gentle forested slopes seen from the mainland. (There is also a toilet just below the summit.)

Return the way you came. While Trig Track provides an alternative circuit back to Rangatira Flat, it is very steep, poorly maintained and very slippery when wet – and doesn't offer anything different to see from the more pleasant Wilkinson Track.

NORTH END

Walks here incorporate Okupe Lagoon, open shrublands and boulder bank, and a loop walk through regenerating forest to a stunning lookout point.

Disembark from the boat and head, as directed by the boat skipper, up off the beach then veer to the right, walk inland for about 150 metres then turn right to the public shelter for your introductory talk.

To continue, follow the signs to Okupe Lagoon and Okupe Loop Track. After about 200 metres from the shelter, passing through a mix of low-growing shrubs, open grassland and young forest, you will come to the first ❸ **southern loop track** junction. You can turn up here if you wish; however, this track passes through more open country and walking in a downhill direction offers better opportunities to appreciate the great outlooks.

After a further 300 metres, beside the lagoon and just before the sprawling boulder bank, the ❹ **northern loop track** turns left and heads uphill through a shady valley, filled with regenerating podocarp forest. Listen here for the tell-tale, high-pitched call announcing the presence of kakariki, red-crowned parakeets.

At the top there is a great ❺ **viewpoint**. Take advantage of the seats, and especially the views. On a good day it's possible to see the mountains of Tongariro National Park. Closer at hand your outlook extends from the Tararua Ranges and across the Horowhenua Plains. The Waikanae River snakes its way from the ranges, meanders through its broad estuary and out to sea. From a conservation point of view there are some good natural and protected habitats here, from the open tussock tops and podocarp and beech forests and rivers of Tararua Forest Park to the wading bird habitat of Waikanae Estuary Scientific Reserve, and then the underground reefs and corals and marine life of Kapiti Marine Reserve that reaches across to Kapiti Island Nature Reserve. Immediately below your vantage point, Okupe Lagoon nestles against the island's northern bouldery coast, and provides a habitat for scaup, grey teal, black swans and sometimes visiting royal spoonbills.

Descend the southern loop track, enjoying the views, and you'll probably still have time to explore the environs of Okupe Lagoon.

The Boulder Bank Loop track continues past the lagoon and two Okupe Loop tracks to the boulder-strewn coastline, then around the very north-eastern tip of the island back to just above your boat-landing point. Shags, gulls, oystercatchers and white-fronted terns will be your likely companions here. Allow an easy hour for the round trip, but note that this coast is closed to public access during bird-breeding season, from November until March.

REFRESHMENTS

There are no shops or cafés on the island, so you will need to pack a picnic, and bring a thermos if you want a hot drink. No fires or camp cookers are permitted on this island nature reserve.

FURTHER READING

Andrew Crowe, *Which Coastal Plant?*, Viking, 1995
Andrew Crowe, *Which Native Fern?*, Viking, 1994
Andrew Crowe, *Which Native Forest Plant?*, Viking, 1999
Andrew Crowe, *Which Native Tree?*, Viking, 1992
Andrew Crowe's books are easy-to-understand guides to common native plants.

Gabites, Isobel, *Wellington's Living Cloak: A guide to the natural plant communities*, Wellington Botanical Society/Victoria University Press, 1993
Everything you might want to know about Wellington's natural vegetation.

Maclean, Chris, *Wellington Telling Tales*, The Whitcombe Press, 2005
Historical and pictorial vignettes of Wellington.

McLean, Gavin, *Wellington: The first years of European settlement 1840-1850*, Penguin, 2000

Off the Eaten Track, Siren Communications Ltd, 1999
This book is an off-the-wall guide to Wellington's best picnic spots.

Wellington Regional Native Plant Guide, Wellington Regional Council, 2000

Wellington Regional Council, the Department of Conservation and each city council produce a comprehensive array of walking and heritage trail brochures.

Other New Zealand titles in the 'Walking ...' series from New Holland Publishers:

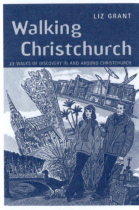

ISBN 978 1 86966 070 3

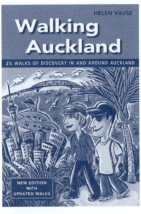

ISBN 978 1 86966 206 6